The New Breed

Alina Hasan

Dedication

For my parents, Nadia and Marwan. And for my
brothers, Dean and Amin.

Acknowledgment

I am thankful to my closest friends, who were my best critics and for pushing me. Most importantly, I am forever grateful to Danielle Darius, who has supported this for five years.

About The Author

Alina Hasan is a young Palestinian-American author. She is a graduate of the University of South Florida, where she received her bachelor's degree in health sciences. She is currently pursuing a master's degree in physician assistant studies at USF.

Contents

Page Left Blank Intentionally

PART ONE

Chapter 1
Felicity

Each day I would wake up from night terrors, drenched in warm sweat. Her face embedded into my everlasting memory. I began to see her horror-filled expression everywhere I turned, in windows and reflections in mirrors. The look would haunt me for the rest of my life.

I reluctantly rolled out of bed and hobbled to the bathroom. My eyes had become swollen and bloodshot from the hours I spent crying in her room. Everything I started to do felt like it was happening in slow-motion. My body was excruciatingly sore, as though I had run a marathon, and I began to look and feel three times my age.

My headaches escalated into migraines, and I caught myself popping Advil constantly. Dust had settled around the house, and dishes were piled up so high, the odor was vile. The blood still stained the wooden floor from my refusal to clean it. I would gag from absolute disgust just from the sight of it. The temperature in the house was at an all-time low. No matter how high I raised the heat, a chilling breeze continued to fill the air. I ignored the possibility that it could be her. I refused to believe it. I spent most of my time searching for small apartments. I couldn't stand the thought of living here without her. Her scent followed me around, and I spent most nights sleeping in her room. Her room was different than mine - quite the opposite. I felt like a teenage boy compared to her, with my rock band posters littering my walls while her floral canvases were neatly placed around the room. Maybe I needed new hobbies to cope with this.

Just in this past week, I had picked up a few unhealthy stress habits such as biting my nails to the nub, scratching my skin until I bled, and biting my lips until they became bloodied. I couldn't help myself. Every time I tried to stop, I would end up doing it without any conscious intention. I threw up about three times a day and was not able to hold anything down. Consequently, I had to eat in the smallest portions one could think of. I felt like a bird - a bird with two broken wings.

Entirely useless.

On a typical Thursday, unlike this one, I would find myself taking a few college classes to complete my bachelor's in literature and afterward, head over to the local bowling alley where I had been working for years.

The bowling alley was small and quaint, and although the pay wasn't great, the staff definitely made up for it. They had become family to me, and I refused to part ways with them. However, at this very moment in time, I couldn't bear the thought of returning and seeing their sympathetic faces. Today, there was a tournament planned that all the pro bowlers in town were participating in. I'd come to know the majority of them and picked up a few tips from them. I wasn't a pro bowler myself, but I was definitely a lot better than the average Joe.

On my days off, I usually took my mom to play a few games and have pizza. She loved the cozy environment. There, everyone knew everyone. The weather today seemed to match my mood; Florida never disappointed with its unexpected thunderstorms. I didn't mind them. The lightning fascinated me. My mom, on the other hand, couldn't stand it. She would always plug in her pink headphones and blare Beyoncé's newest release until she completely blocked out the bellowing thunder. The sight never failed to make me laugh. Sometimes, I questioned deep down if our roles were switched, and I was actually the mom. Our lives seemed like we were the stars of *Freaky Friday*. I was definitely the more responsible one, and sometimes, she would call me "Mom" or respond with, "Yes, mother."

I stared at my reflection in the shattered mirror, cringing. I smashed it out of anger the night after everything happened, and never got around to cleaning up the shards of glass. This girl was unrecognizable, a stranger. Her brunette hair was matted and disheveled in all directions, under-eyes so dark and puffy that no amount of makeup could hide it, and her wrinkled black dress stopped just short of her knees. Her olive skin was completely washed out, and her purple veins were prominent from a lack of nutrition. She looked like a tragic mess. And well, she was.

Sighing, I threw my hair up into a messy bun and added a large headband to conceal the knotted disaster. The house was dark. I hadn't turned on a light in a week, hoping I wouldn't have to see any memories and face the truth. I was in denial, praying that this was all just a sick nightmare that I would wake up from, eventually. But I knew I was wrong. I knew I was wrong when I banged my head on the concrete wall for hours, trying to wake myself up. I knew I was wrong when I held her in my arms, when the crimson blood seeped into my own white cotton t-shirt, dyeing it in a new hue. I knew I was wrong. I just refused to believe it.

The toast and strawberry jam I ate for breakfast tasted bland. Nothing tasted the same anymore; nothing I did was the same anymore. I refused to answer the numerous phone calls from friends and neighbors who wanted to check up on me. They were all really just interested in the story and the events of that horrible night, so they could share their newfound information the police refused to reveal.

So instead, I took the battery out of my cell phone, shut all the blinds in the house, and completely isolated myself.

"It's just a phase." They convinced me.

"It gets easier." They lied.

Some nights I couldn't shut off my brain; I couldn't stop thinking about it all. At times like this, I pulled out the blenders we used to make smoothies and milkshakes and turned them on simultaneously.

Then I couldn't hear it... the voices.

Then I couldn't see it... the memories.

And that was better for me.

I slipped on a pair of giant sunglasses in an attempt to mask my face and started my maroon '68 Pontiac Firebird. It was my father's before he died and was now my most prized possession. To ever get rid of that car would be like tearing a chunk of my heart out from my chest.

Even though I never truly knew my dad or even saw pictures of him, I always felt like he was riding shotgun with me. I would blast rock music and pretend he was singing along with me, even though I had no idea what his voice sounded like. It gave me a little peace of mind, but also a longing for him. But today was not one of those days. There would be no jamming to rock music or having fun, or thinking of what could have been.

Only of what was.

My vision blurred the entire car ride making the stoplights seem five times bigger, and the other cars on the road five times closer. It felt like I forgot to pop in my contacts.

I was in a daze. Cars and trucks zoomed by while I passed her favorite Greek restaurant and the flower market she often visited. Then came the blueberry fields we loved to stop over at. We always ended up with way more than what we needed, so we would make muffins for our friends.

Everyone knew her. Everyone loved her.

When I arrived at the funeral home, everyone was already there. I was late to my own mother's wake. I prayed she wouldn't be mad, as we were always "fashionably late," she called it. As I entered through the decorative glass doors, I felt everyone's gaze shift toward me, making me instantly uncomfortable.

I quietly cleared my throat to get their attention.

"Thank you all for coming, it means a lot to me as well as my mom." I aimed my eyes at the patterned, carpeted ground, not daring to look up. After a few awkward moments of silence, the guests continued to roam around and gossip.

My body was numb throughout my mother's wake and service. The constant apologies and pity I received was pure torture. I spent most of my time hiding in the bathroom or sneaking outside so the rain could drown their chatter.

"Did you hear it was suicide?"

"Poor Alice found her dying. A knife in her stomach."

"It's a shame she left her daughter on her own."

"She has no one left; that was the last of her family."

"You know suicide leads straight to hell? It's in the Bible!"

I couldn't stand their crude remarks that they whispered amongst each other. So instead, I stood outside protected by the covering of the peeling roof, and played with my mom's old lighter, sticking my fingers into the flame.

It was a game we used to play when I was younger. We would light candles around the house and swipe our fingers through them. It never burned, and it was the first time I saw her wilder side.

She said she used to do it to scare her mom.

Poor Grandma.

Grandma died when I was three, so I have no memories of her. Sometimes, I could smell sweet peppermint in the house. That was the way mom described her, like a candy cane.

The rain was falling slower and quieter, and I could see a rainbow peeking between the clouds. The red was the most prominent color. Mom's favorite color.

The color of the lipstick she wore.

The color of the blood she had.

The color that now stained my white shirt.

Yet, something had seized my mind, making it impossible to focus at all. Flashbacks of the night it all happened replayed like a movie in my head. The one thing I had kept from the police that held some answers to this misery. The one thing that could possibly assist me in uncovering the truth.

The letter.

The letter that was now splattered with her blood, hidden in my pillowcase on my bed. I reread it over a thousand times this past week. Each time, things were making less and less sense. Half of the words began to smear beneath my shower of tears, making the cursive illegible. Eventually, I pulled myself together and continued to mourn her death with the others.

Despite the odds, I somehow managed to get to the cemetery in one piece. The rain had finally stopped, leaving the earth soft and mushy. Mud attached itself to the leather of my shoes. I tried to force a small smile on my face as thanks to the group of people who had shown up, but my mouth was latched shut, and as much as I tried, it wouldn't release. So instead, I gave a slight curt nod to everyone who passed, trying to seem appreciative.

Avoiding their stares, I took my place near my mother's cherry wooden coffin. The cemetery was small and crowded with hundreds of other graves. The grass had replaced its lush green color for a brown, emphasizing all of the death that occupied the area. The rain was much needed. Goosebumps replaced any smooth skin on my body, and I held myself for warmth.

The spirits that lurked around mixed with the wind of autumn made me regret not grabbing a jacket on my way out. The place honestly just made my skin crawl. I blocked out all the prayers and speeches that people gave, pretending like they actually knew my mother. Like they actually knew what she had been through... what we had been through.

And at the end, when they all expected me to talk, to say how much I loved and missed her, I shook my head, placed her favorite daisies on her coffin, and walked away. She always loved their simplicity and pure color. They made her happier in general, and all I truly wanted was for her to be happy where she was going.

The daisies reminded me of her. Simple. But sometimes, they would surprise you and blossom into magnificent, cheerful pink daisies. And that was exactly like her, surprising.

The pain in my heart was too much to bear.

As I quickly attempted to flee the scene, I saw someone who I never expected to see in a million years. I had to do a double-take. The person who I had tucked far and deep inside of my brain and blocked off with "Caution, Danger!" tape. The person who I had finally forgotten about.

The person whose fault it was that my mother cried herself to sleep for years. Rage immediately flooded my emotions, and I could sense my face turning a heated sunburn red. If it were possible, steam would have definitely been coming out of my ears and fire from my mouth. The fact that this man had the decency to show up at my mother's funeral after he left us all those years ago, abandoned, absolutely boiled my blood. I marched over to the epitome of Satan, whom I refused to think of as my uncle, as family, or as of the same blood.

"What are you doing here?" I hissed, making sure there was no one around to witness the nauseating reunion. He looked so different from when I last saw him five years ago. I was fifteen at the time. He looked so different, yet exactly the same. When you've known someone practically your whole life, they become too recognizable to forget. His metal gray eyes, which were similar to mine, contained the same silver flecks they always had, but their spark was gone. His hair was in the same layered cut he'd been getting for years, but it was shaggier than it used to be.

The scruff on his face clearly indicated he still only shaved once a week. He was still tall as ever at a towering 6'2", and remained as lean and fit as I could remember from the runs he forced me to join him on. However, it was clear to me that he had aged. The gray that streaked through his dark chocolate-mousse colored hair was a sure sign, and the purple circles beneath his eyes were nearly as bad as mine. I wondered what could be keeping him up at night.

The guilt?

"Honestly, I kind of expected a hug." He half smirked at me shoving his hands in the pockets of his navy colored jeans.

He wore a simple black polo and a silver watch.

The silver watch.

The one with the engraved roman numerals.

The one I had saved up all of my babysitting money to buy for him on his thirty-fifth birthday. I wondered if he had worn it on purpose, as a peace offering. But there would be no peace with him. Not today, not ever. I remembered the jokes we had and all of the pranks we pulled, and I wanted to laugh and forgive him, but then I recalled why I couldn't. Why I could never forgive him. The countless nights I went without any sleep taking care of my mom. Blowing up his phone when he left us when he disappeared with no explanation. The depression she went through because of him. The numerous pills she was forced to take.

He was the reason for it all, and I was not a forgiving person. "You can't be serious! After all that you've done? Everything you put her through! Everything you put me through!" I was beyond furious; I was enraged. At this point, I was prepared to dig a grave for him myself. "You left us! No goodbyes or phone calls. Nothing! Or have you forgotten?" He looked at me in utter shock and disbelief. Regret filled every pore of his face.

"Alice, listen, you don't understand-"

Before I gave him a chance to come up with an excuse I'd never believe, I cut him off.

"Listen to me. I never want to see you again, ever. Get out of here right now before I call the police. And don't you dare come back here." I used my best efforts to sound commanding and threatening, but when it's coming from a petite girl who's only 5'4, it's hard to be that convincing.

I stomped away, crunching the dead grass beneath my worn-out leather ankle boots and ignored his pathetic, useless calls. My lips quivered like a baby's who had bumped his head on the edge of a table.

I ran toward my car, head down, not wanting anyone to read the frustration on my face. I counted the seconds it was taking me to reach the security of my vehicle, only to make sudden contact with the muddy ground.

"Shit!" I mumbled as I pushed myself up.

I looked at the man I had run into and apologized. "I'm sorry. I wasn't looking where I was going."

He was wearing a fancy black suit and tie; the kind businessmen wore. He looked happy. Not the type of emotion one expressed at a cemetery.

"It's not a problem." He laughed. "Are you sure you're okay?"

"My dress won't be, but I'm fine." I smiled and walked the remaining distance to my car, being careful not to make another embarrassing scene.

I tried to wipe the wet mud off the back of my dress, not wanting to get the Firebird's tan leather seats dirty.

I could imagine him at the moment, watching, laughing as he remembered how clumsy I was.

I looked down at my hand, realizing my ring was missing. It was a silver band with my name engraved into it that my mom had gotten me for my 18th birthday. I turned to go back to retrieve it from where I fell.

What I saw made me refuse to go back.

The man in the suit was knelt down, with his back facing me, picking up my ring. As he bent forward, his suit jacket lifted, revealing a black pistol.

And that's when I knew he wasn't visiting a loved one.

That's when I knew he wasn't a businessman.

I quickly hopped into my car, ignoring his desperate waves for me to stop, and for the second time that day, I fled the scene.

Chapter 2
The Letter

A yellow bolt of lightning illuminated my room through the window, followed by a loud crack of thunder. The thunderstorms had started up again. When I returned home from the dreadful yet frightening funeral, I put my racing mind on hold and searched for her letter.

It was still inside of my blue pillowcase, folded into a thousand tiny squares. Pulling out the letter immediately made my stomach sink. Remembering the events of that night after returning home from work at the bowling alley caused me to be sick.

I quickly grabbed the trash bin next to my bed to empty the contents of my stomach. Every time I closed my eyes, I could vividly remember walking into the kitchen to ask Mom what she wanted for dinner, only to be met with her lifeless body on the floor next to a kitchen knife. I shook my head to rid the memory.

Dear Alice,

I'm sorry you had to find me like this. I've only ever wanted for you to have a better life. Maybe with me out of the way, you can make something out of yourself. Promise me you'll make something of yourself?

I need you to understand something so that you can move on. Your father, he was a bad man. He did a lot of bad things to a lot of good people. Some men might come for you. Go with them, they can help.

Don't trust anyone, and be careful.

I'll love you for eternity,

Mom.

My eyes were glued to the lined paper.

Something was very wrong.

As I examined the writing a bit more, I noticed something in the middle paragraph. Her y's and g's weren't looped. She *always* looped her y's and g's; it was her signature. Whenever she left me a note in the kitchen or wrote on my napkins for lunch in elementary school, everything was looped.

But something even stranger - besides the middle paragraph, everything else seemed to be written in her handwriting. Unlike the rest of the letter, the cursive in the middle paragraph seemed to be forced and hurried.

Letters didn't connect smoothly, and things looked shaky.

I *had* to notice these differences. They could give me the answers I was looking for. More perplexed and agitated than I had already been, I stuffed the letter back inside my pillowcase and decided to do some digging the next day.

Before I could allow myself to enter the underworld, I concerned myself with the man in the suit at the funeral. This paranoia forced me to leave the comfort of my bed and lock all windows and doors, shut down all blinds and curtains, turn on the house alarm, and grab a kitchen knife for my nightstand drawer.

I was not taking *any* chances.

And I was *definitely* not going with any man that came for me.

I was going to make something of myself.

Mom requested it.

The harsh rays of the sun streamed through my curtains, blinding me. As much as I wanted to stay in bed all day and grieve like I had been doing for the last week, I knew it was time to do something.

The first thing I needed to do was move. Move away from this house and the dangers it could bring me. I refused to believe that my mother's death was a suicide. And if I was right, then her murderer would be back again, and I was not going to stay to find out. Moving wasn't as simple as you would think. You can't just grab your things and leave. Our attic was filled to the brim with boxes that I never had the chance to go through. I wasn't going to allow some stranger to move into this house with my family's secrets lying around.

I was going to have to go through everything one by one, being careful not to throw any valuable things out. It could be rent money, dinner money, or maybe even answers. I grabbed a flashlight and stared at the door that led to the attic. I had never been a fan of dark and spooky places, and the attic hadn't been touched in years, so I expected some sort of mutant rodent to be crawling around.

Sighing, I placed the flashlight in my mouth as I pulled the door down from the ceiling and climbed the ladder that descended. Each step creaked, increasing my fear of falling off the ladder. The light hadn't been replaced in years, so I could only depend on my flashlight.

Once I reached the top, I sat at the edge and scanned the attic. Everything was covered in a thick layer of dust. I realized then that this was a two-person job. I couldn't grab a box, climb down, climb back up, and repeat; it would all take too long, and I would definitely fall while trying to balance.

As I debated whether or not I should call a friend, I heard a bang near the back of the house. I quickly descended the steps to the attic and hid behind a couch in the living room, since it was the only thing I had time to get to. The back door opened, and heavy footsteps sounded on the wooden floor.

"Hello?" The voice called out.

I instantly recognized it.

Gathering myself up off of the ground, I went to confront him.

"Are you crazy?" I asked my so-called "uncle," James, in utter disbelief.

"I thought you were a serial killer!"

I was beyond furious. First, he shows up at my mother's funeral, and now he breaks into my house. He's crossed way too many lines.

"Alice, I still have this." He pulled out the house key we had made for him years ago.

"Doesn't mean you're still welcome here!" I crossed my arms and stood my ground. "You have five seconds before I call the police," I warned him.

"You're not going to do that." He countered.

"And why is that?" I uncrossed my arms, preparing to sprint to my room for my phone. For all I know, he could have killed my mom. After a five-year mysterious disappearance, he suddenly returns right after my mom's death... what could possibly sound more suspicious than that? "We need to talk. About your mom." He shifted uncomfortably and pulled at the end of his brown leather jacket nervously. The same one he wore over five years ago. The leather was beyond worn out.

After a few awkward moments of silence, I reluctantly sat on the white couch to hear what he had to say.

He sat across from me in a chair leaned over.

"What happened to her... she didn't do it. It wasn't suicide. It couldn't have been." His thoughts were unorganized. He clearly hadn't practiced his speech before arriving.

As much as I believed his accusations, I had to dig deeper.

"What makes you think that?" I asked, pretending to be shocked. The look on his face showed uncertainty and sadness. It couldn't have been him. He was family for god sake.

"Family"

What a powerful word that is supposed to mean so much, but truthfully means nothing.

"The thing is, I can't exactly tell you everything. Not yet, at least. But I want you to know that she didn't kill herself."

Are you kidding me? He came all the way over here to tell me that he can't tell me anything.

"Well, as much as I'd love for you to stay and chat over some lunch, I'd really appreciate it if you left. Permanently." I stood from the couch, motioning towards the door, fists clenched.

Breathe Alice, breathe.

One. Two. Three. Four. Five. Six. Seven. Eight. Nine. Ten.

"Alice, you don't have to be like this." He looked hurt, upset, and frustrated.

"No, *James*. I do have to be like this. I have been like this, and it's your fault. I don't need you coming in to disrupt my life." I began ranting to him, trying to rid myself of him and the memories he brought.

More like misfortunes.

James. I called him James. Not Uncle like I used to.

"You don't understand Alice-"

"You're right! I don't understand! I don't understand why you left us, why you disappeared, and why suddenly you're back now!" I shouted at him, tears brimming my eyes. I refused to let them fall. I refused to let him see me cry.

After standing in the background listening to my rage, he finally interrupted.

"I was protecting you both! There are these people, they wanted to kill me, so I had to leave. If they found me, they would have found you both. I didn't know this was going to happen. I didn't know they were going to find Felicity." Felicity. Mom. Mother. Mama. Mommy.

So many names for one human being.

One human being who is now six feet underground.

Six feet buried deep.

Gone.

I leaned back in my seat and washed a hand over my face, refusing to acknowledge what he just said. There were people after him? Why? I had so many questions but was not fond of hearing their answers come from James. Especially since he just openly admitted to being the reason for her death.

I got up and walked to the kitchen to brew myself a cup of coffee to get rid of the migraine beginning to turn up. James' footsteps sounded behind me in the kitchen. He wore dark brown heavy work boots. Not the shoes a typical person would go for. But then again, he wasn't a typical person.

"If you're going to stay, I need answers, not bullshit about keeping me safe." I stated firmly, turning to face him. "Otherwise, you're useless and just in the way." My heart was still wrapped in a thick sheet of ice. Cold.

He shoved his hands in his jacket pockets and nodded. "Okay. You got it."

"First things first. We've got to get out of here, so help me go through the attic." I sipped the last of my coffee and placed it in the sink.

James was soon up the ladder and handing me boxes. Once the attic had been cleared, we got to work.

"Anything that looks the least bit suspicious, give it to me." I sat on the floor crisscross and opened the first box that I saw. The first hour of going through the boxes had been a huge waste of time. There were just little knickknacks and keepsakes Mom never wanted to get rid of.

I sighed and leaned against the wall, ready to give up as a splitting headache was coming on. I groaned and felt the blood rush to my nose, and the usual trickle oozed down to my lip. "You still get those?" James asked, furrowing his brows.

I'd been getting nosebleeds since I was a baby, and they never seemed to get any better. The doctor said they were probably just a symptom of seasonal allergies.

Probably.

Probably wasn't going to cut it from now on.

I mumbled a "yeah" and went to wash my face, which was now stained red. When I walked back to the boxes, James was curiously looking at a picture.

"What is it?" I asked, walking over to him.

"Nothing, it's just a picture." He folded it in half and tucked it away in the box.

"James." I held out my hand for the picture, knowing he was hiding something.

"It's nothing." He tried to reassure me.

"Damnit! I'm trying to figure out what happened to her, and you're not helping much!" I yanked the picture out of the box with white knuckles. The back of the picture said 'Alice Avery, November '94'. A month after I was born. I anxiously unfolded the picture to reveal me at one-month-old, laying on an operating table with tubes and wires decorating my tiny body. In horror, I threw the picture at James.

"What is this? What the hell is this?" I demanded an answer. No one ever told me of any surgeries I had to go through. What was wrong with me?

"You're going to have to sit down for this one." He warned me, walking over to the couches.

I reluctantly followed him and sat.

"The company your mother and I worked for, called Mandala, performed experiments..." He began.

"The first one ever performed was done on you."

I gasped in shock. How could they let this happen? My own family?

"It was for your own good. You were having pains and always crying. It was to help you." He explained.

"Pains? I don't feel pain." I had never felt pain throughout my entire life... that I could remember at least. And then it all clicked. My mom told me I was diagnosed with Congenital Insensitivity to Pain when I was younger. I was supposedly the only survivor with this disorder.

That was the experiment they performed on me.

I was stunned.

The room looked like it was spinning and my head felt like it weighed a thousand pounds.

"I think that's enough for today," I stated while rubbing my temples. "I'm going for a jog."

Before he could lecture me again about my safety, I was already out the door and tying my sneakers. I had to get away from him and the house to clear my mind.

Chapter 3
The Experiments

Hundreds of questions were rushing through my brain. If I was the first person they experimented on, that means there were other experiments too. And then came the question about what types of experiments they performed. Clearly, they had the ability to change bodily functions, and that could do some damage.

My mind was wandering around so many questions, creating a headache and disturbing my current reality. The evening Florida sky was painted pink like cotton candy, mesmerizing and distracting me from the catastrophic reality headed my way. I focused on the pattern of my breathing and the sound of each heel lightly patting the pavement. I was using all my efforts to avoid having to confront my future but failing miserably.

I was being consumed in what if's and hypothetical scenarios. I continued down a trail through the woods just as the sun was setting. The leaves crunched under my sneakers, masking any other sound of wildlife... or human life. Two miles into the trail, and a heavy suspicion clouded my judgment. My head snapped in each direction, trying to detect the slightest sounds and movements coming from the trees. I made a sharp turn to head back home, and just as my neck whipped around, I noticed a black figure rushing behind a tree. I gasped for air and ran full speed back to the direction I came from, never once looking back.

"Get home, get home, get home, get home." This was repeating in my mind like a broken record.

I just needed to get home.

My breathing became so intense I felt as though I were hyperventilating. If I were someone else, by now, my shins would be aching from not running in a long time, and my chest would be burning. But I could not feel anything, so I continued running. I tried to focus on the sound of my sneakers, crushing the leaves and nothing else.

Running had always been my escape since I wasn't permitted to play in any team sports. The possibility and risks of me getting injured and not realizing it was too high. Any sense of internal bleeding, headaches, and pains I couldn't detect could prove to be life-threatening, and no one would ever know. Under a physician's orders, I was forbidden from all sports, except running. Once my house became visible, I noticed James getting in his car to leave. The fear of abandonment struck me again. Not again, he cannot leave me again.

"No! No! James, no!" I wailed while flailing my arms and sprinting toward him.

I reached him before he entered his car, completely out of breath and exhausted from my possibly imaginary chase.

"James, we have to leave now." I managed to escape the most important thing I needed to say. Without asking any questions, he shoved the remaining boxes in my trunk, and we headed off in our separate cars, with me following him blindly. I had no idea where he would lead me, but anything felt better than being "home."

I never thought I would feel that leaving home was necessary for my survival. After driving for a little over an hour through the night, we finally arrived at a small lone cabin surrounded by skyscraping trees deep in the woods. The cabin was much less luxurious than one would imagine. It was rundown, with the front porch held together by a few wooden floorboards and nothing else. I made no comment and abided by James' advice to hop from the last stair to the front door. Once "safely" inside with my boxes, I took a deep breath and collapsed onto the dust-filled couch. I was exhausted and vulnerable and needed to share.

"I think there was someone following me."

James washed his face over with his hands, "Damnit, they found us."

All I wanted to do was scream. "Who are they?" What did my mom and her brother do that was so bad that "they" are after us? After me?

I was too drained to even press for more information. My body was shutting down from dehydration and insomnia. The stiff couch suddenly felt like a cloud, and as my heavy eyelids drooped, all my problems seemingly disappeared, and I was taken under. I certainly needed it as well. My body was in a field of daisies, lying on the grass, feeling the warmth of the sun on my skin. I was aware that I was dreaming, but I wasn't able to wake myself up. I didn't want to be surrounded by daisies, and I didn't want to think anymore. At least, while I was dreaming.

It felt unfair to be tortured in both real life and dream life. I was supposed to escape my hellish reality once my eyes closed. Despite my apparent mental argument with the universe, my dream continued. I heard movement in the forest beyond me, so I quickly rolled onto my stomach to get a better look.

Approximately ten feet from my position was a beautiful deer with antlers as intricate as the roots of oaks. We made direct eye contact as it slowly made its way toward me. I rose from my position on the ground, unsure if I should reach out and touch the deer, or slowly back away. Just as I made the decision to pet the beautiful creature, an arrow pierced its skull just as fast as I had blinked. The deer collapsed into the beautiful field of daisies, blood seeping from its head as I screamed out in anger.

I turned towards the woods attempting to locate the source of the murderer, but only caught a glimpse of the black figure I had seen in my own woods; in my own reality. I knelt down to the dying deer and felt no other urge except to apologize as if its death was my fault. Everything felt like my fault. I wept until its eyes finally shut, signaling its end. I wanted to break free from this dream, but my eyes were sealed shut. I searched the open field with tear-stained eyes, thinking I could find a way to escape. There was a cliff nearby... and a person?

Someone was running towards the cliff. Was it my mom?

"Mom?"

"Mom!" I yelled out, waiting for her to turn around, just wanting to get one last look at her face.

I was sure it was her now, the way she ran swaying side to side gave it away. But why was she running towards the cliff?

"Run."

That was the only thought that came into my mind.

"Mom!" I continued to shout as I ran toward her.

She was nearing the edge, but I was gaining on her.

The daisies that littered the field suddenly died and turned an ash color, as they crumpled under my bare feet. The once blue sky was now consumed in dark gray clouds. The whole environment was changing. Something terrible was going to happen.

I finally reached the edge just behind my mom. I was too scared to touch her as if she'd go through my fingertips, and then I'd lose her. She was wearing a plain white dress. It looked like she wrapped our curtains around her, but she seemed effortlessly beautiful in the darkness that now gripped us. She slowly turned toward me, and just as I got a look at her pale face, an arrow shot right through her stomach, where she allegedly stabbed herself.

The power of the arrow struck her off the cliff, forcing her to fall backward. She yelled my name as her white torso became soaked in blood. I could only watch in horror as her body fell towards the river below that was filled with rocks. Her body struck a rock with a loud thrash, and I shrieked out in pain… too loud, I guess.

The next thing I knew, James was holding a cold, damp towel to my forehead. I was finally awake and aware of the tears that had streaked down my face during my nightmare.

"Felicity?" He asked in a knowing tone.

I nodded, unable to form coherent sentences. The sunlight streamed in through the little window above the kitchen sink, illuminating the small cabin that resembled a prison cell. It was morning, and although I slept through the entire night, I felt incredibly unrested. Despite my sleep deprivation, I knew there was work to be done. I was determined to solve my mother's murder.

The only problem to this was being a 20-year-old, vulnerable, 5'4" girl who only knew how to run. It was time I found out who I was dealing with and what needed to be done. It was time to plan what I needed to do. I took a quick, cold shower with little to no water pressure and was ready to discuss a plan. I was prepared to fight. When I emerged from the bathroom, James was preparing two cups of coffee as if he remembered how I took mine...

which he did. Him being the adult, and me having no faith in myself, resulted in my automatic assumption that he should have all the answers to this disaster and know exactly what to do. I forgot how cross I was with him. Unfortunately, to my dismay, he was of little help and only knew about the past, and the fact that he had been running from the company ever since. "The company is not just a facility that you can track down. They have several facilities planted all over the world in underground bunkers that can potentially never be found. They're not to be messed with. We just need to keep on the run," I sat with my mouth agape, angry at his dismal reply.

"They murdered your sister!" I shouted in anger.

"How can you be satisfied with staying hidden? We need to do something about this!" I was in utter disbelief.

"Alice, I'm not satisfied. This company is bigger than you think and will ruin us a lot easier than you think." James tried to reason with me, but revenge was the only thing on my mind. Revenge, which can easily cloud your judgment.

"Is this where you've been hiding?" I pondered aloud, ignoring his negativity.

"One of the places, yes." He responded, running his hand through his wavy brunette hair.

"So, there are more?" I raised my eyebrows, curious.

He nodded, not catching onto where my idea was headed.

"We can easily make "The Company" think we're someplace that we're not." I used air quotes to emphasize the fact that I was unamused by them. I was ready to strategize.

At first, James had a look of awe on his face, but it quickly changed when he realized what we were getting ourselves into.

"Alice, this isn't a good idea. This is a world of trouble we're going to get ourselves into." He warned.

"Well I have nothing left to lose, do you?" Although this statement was probably untrue, being at the ripe age of 20 and having an entire lifetime ahead of me, I was prepared to drop everything for this cause. This was too big, and I didn't want anyone else being tested on or losing a loved one as I did.

"Alright, let's get started." He reluctantly agreed, and I smiled at him for the first time in years. The smile felt distant but familiar, a warm feeling. A feeling of being with family. However, I had to remind myself that he could leave again, and I needed to be prepared for that.

"First thing's first. We need to go through the boxes again and throw away anything we don't need. We can't have anything holding us down." He agreed, and we got to digging.

Most of the things we discovered in the boxes were useless. We agreed to only save one box for memorabilia and hide it as best as possible so that it didn't get damaged during our entire ordeal. After sorting through the boxes for what seemed to be an eternity, I came across a small photo album that contained pictures of dozens of babies and children. Before I even had to ask, I knew what it was. James explained that these were pictures of all the children they worked with that were tested on with various diseases and disorders around the same time as me.

This got me thinking.

"So, there are more like me? That means they're either the same age as me or older. What if they could help us? We have to find them." My mind was racing with endless possibilities of the future.

"Alice you have to realize a lot of them are dead. It's a good idea, but many experiments failed so we'll probably only be able to find a few. And on top of that, there's a great possibility they don't even know what's been done to them. Are you willing to ruin that?"

I didn't even have to think. I was being selfish. Of course, I was willing to ruin that. I was doing this for my mom, and I reasoned in my mind that they should be aware of what's happened to them. I left James at the cabin to continue digging through boxes while I set out to the nearest library with the photo album to start some research.

Chapter 4
The Others

After only a ten-minute drive, I reached a local public library. It was a lot bigger than I expected, but I assumed it was probably because it was near a university. I grabbed my bag that contained the photo album and set out, determined to find people to help. The vastness of the library was intimidating.

Several floors of shelves filled with books and college students studying. I missed school and studying, but I realized it wasn't my focus anymore. My situation is now, college can be later. I made my way towards the section with computers and settled in. I knew I'd be here awhile. I pulled out my notebooks and pens and noticed how empty my hand felt without my ring.

A few minutes after I began my scavenger hunt, a girl who looked to be some years younger than myself sat directly across from me. She had long strawberry blonde hair and large brown rimmed glasses. She smiled politely at me, and I assumed she'd get back to her work, but she wanted to chat.

"Hi, I'm Felicity." The strawberry blonde introduced herself.

Felicity. Her name was Felicity. I had never met another Felicity before in my entire existence.

I bit down on my lip hard.

"Alice." I smiled and immediately turned back to my computer, stomach aching. It seemed she knew that I was uncomfortable, so she left me unbothered.

At least for a little while.

Only fifteen minutes later, and barely into my research, she interrupted again.

"Studying?" She asked as she typed on her computer.

"Yeah." I nodded, "Lots of finals coming up." Instant regret. Finals weren't for another two months what was I thinking.

She raised her eyebrows a little at my obvious lie but continued the conversation.

"Do you go here?" The stranger with my mother's name asked, referring to the college nearby. My lie definitely raised some red flags. I decided to spare myself the embarrassment this time and just tell the truth.

"No, I go to a community college, I'm just visiting."

This sparked her interest and her obvious problem of procrastination, so Felicity and I ended up getting to know each other for the duration I was there.

I was a little annoyed that she was distracting me from much more important things, but it was nice to have some human interaction, especially since she reminded me of my friends back home. Once she finished her work, she gathered her things and headed to my side of the table. She leaned over and jotted her number down in my notebook while I quickly minimized the screen that I was on.

She noticed this reaction and slightly laughed at me, while waving goodbye and being on her way. I watched as she left the library, curious about her confidence and our interaction. Did I just make a new friend? I shook the idea out of my head. I'm too busy for friends.

I set out to do exactly what I came for, undistracted this time. There were only twenty pictures in the photo album. Assuming the majority were dead, this shouldn't take too long. I began with the first picture, Danny Ables, 14 months, Schizophrenia.

"Jesus!" I exclaimed at the thought of having schizophrenia and received a few evil looks from students deep in their studying. Perhaps, I was a bit loud in my exclamation. After an extensive search on the internet, Danny Ables appeared to be dead. I crossed his picture off the list, not knowing if it was for better or for worse.

Next.

This process repeated for two more hours while I continuously scratched one name after the other off the list. My heart hurt. All of these innocent babies and children dead, just for experimentation.

Just when I was about to give up, I got a hit on Amy Fells. She was five when she was experimented on, and the company gave her Alzheimer's. Fantastic.

I tried to focus on the positives since she was the first one I found alive. I wrote down her number and address and continued onto the last five names, crossing my fingers that I'd at least get one more hit. Better yet, two hits. Zeke Harris and Zoe Knight. Zeke was six when he was given a cardiovascular disease, congestive heart failure; Zoe was three when she received leukemia.

I quickly jotted down their phone numbers and addresses and gathered my things. I had spent too much time at the library, only finding three people. The number of baby pictures I had to cross off made my hands shake, and I needed to get back to the cabin. Unfortunately, only Zeke lived in Florida. Zoe lived in North Carolina, and Amy lived in New Jersey. This meant Zeke was the first on my list. Zeke also had the highest potential among all the hits because of his age.

On my car ride back to the cabin, I pondered over the best possible tactic to befriend these strangers. Should I call and embarrass myself on the phone, while trying to explain the nonsense of the situation? Or do I show up to their houses, probably frightening them into thinking I had a psych disorder? Once I reached the cabin, I decided it would probably be best to confront these people in person. Maybe I could provide evidence to convince them that I'm not crazy. Doing this over the phone would be too difficult. Although I hardly believed I had any convincing evidence. I entered by hopping from the last stair to the doorstep, avoiding the porch just like James had told me. I found him sitting on the dusty couch staring at a blank TV screen, probably sipping his third cup of coffee for the day.

"What took you so long?" He glanced at me.

"We're going on a road trip," I bluntly stated while packing the few items I now owned into a backpack.

"And we're taking the Firebird," I added.

James walked over and picked up my backpack holding it over his head. I felt like a child again being compared to his height.

"We're not going anywhere until you explain." James retorted.

I was slightly annoyed that he wouldn't just listen to me and agree to everything I was saying, but I guess it was good that he was there to keep me level headed. I elaborated to him about the three people that I found that were still alive, and how we needed to go and pay each of them a visit. When he finally agreed, he helped me pack, and we were ready to be on our way.

Our first stop, Jacksonville, Florida.

My chest was tight with anticipation, and my mind filled with curiosity and doubt. What if the address was wrong? What if he's not there? Too much room for error and things to go wrong, I guess.

Jacksonville was only about a four-hour drive from the cabin, so we split the driving in half.

During my two-hour rest period, I decided to text Felicity from the library to take my mind off things and occupy my time. In reality, I should have been planning what to say to Zeke, but I just couldn't bring myself to do it yet. In fact, I wanted to avoid that for as long as possible.

I was trying to imagine a world post this situation and considered the possibility of being friends with Felicity. She immediately responded to my text, and we struck up a conversation about ourselves. Well, mainly me since she was asking most of the questions. It began to feel more like an interrogation. It reminded me of playing 20 questions in middle school.

Once our conversation seemed to be hitting a dead end, I received a peculiar message from her.

"So where are you headed?"

I hadn't given her any clues or hints that I was going somewhere in particular. It was as if she knew where I was. I was definitely spooked, so I stopped responding hoping to avoid another potentially threatening situation. The only perk to the odd conversation was that it helped my last two hours fly by. Within no time, we were parked outside of Zeke's house and the realization that I still had no idea what to say hit me. I found that I was unprepared and had no idea how to go forward with Zeke.

"Are you ready?" James asked shutting the car off.

"No, I'm not ready!" I blurted out.

"Sorry," I whispered following my outburst.

"I just didn't think this through. I need a minute."

So there we sat in silence, while I pretended to think of what to say to Zeke, even though in reality, I was just going to wing it.

After five minutes went by, I opened the car door, signaling that I was ready.

"Do you want me to come?" James asked still seated in the driver's seat. I contemplated letting him join for moral support but decided against it when I realized James would probably intimidate the situation.

"Maybe I should talk to him alone," I explained, since I looked pretty harmless. At least physically. He nodded, agreeing, and watched me walk up to the door.

The house was a large, two-story white picket fence type house that you see in the movies whenever the quarterback of the high school football team throws a party. There were no cars in the driveway which made my stomach tie into knots. If Zeke wasn't home, it would put the entire plan on hold.

I finally rang the doorbell and stared blankly at the royal blue front door, while I closely listened to the echo of the doorbell. It seemed as though I was waiting for centuries before the door swung open.

"Hello?" The man asked furrowing his brows.

It was precisely how Zeke looked in the pictures on the internet.

"Hi, um. Hi, I'm Alice." I stuttered over my words.

"I was wondering if I could talk to you about your past maybe?" It came out as a very confused question. I really should have thought this through.

"You want to talk about my past?" He said with a slight chuckle, while slowly closing the door on me.

"Well, more specifically your medical condition," I stated more assertively, sticking my foot in the door.

Zeke's surprised look made me regret coming off so harshly.

"I'm sorry, we just really need to talk." I apologized hoping he would offer me into his home.

As soon as I thought he might, he peered out and saw James suspiciously sitting in the car.

"Shit," I muttered under my breath.

Zeke shoved my foot from inside his home and slammed the door shut.

"I don't know who you are, but I'm going to call the cops in one minute if you and your friend aren't gone!" Zeke shouted from behind his door.

"Zeke wait! Do you know about Mandala?" This was my last shot. I didn't know if this guy knew anything about his past or the truth about his condition, but it was the only chance I had to actually get him to hear me out. Silence. One minute of silence went by before the door finally cracked open.

"How do you know about Mandala?" He asked quietly as if anyone could be listening.

"I was experimented on, too." I sighed with a hand on the door refusing to let him slam it on me again. He swung the door open wider and motioned for me to enter. I gave James a thumbs up behind my back to let him know I was okay.

Once inside Zeke's house, I paced around while he grabbed himself a glass of water. The entire house was white except for the dark, hardwood floorboards. The rug was white, the couch, the walls, and the coffee table too. I felt as though my mere presence dirtied the entire area, considering I'd been shacked up in a cabin in the middle of the woods and was dressed in all black. My hair was matted from a lack of proper shampoo and water pressure, and my dark under-eyes made me look as if I'd been punched in the face in a fight. I was dressed in black jeans, a black t-shirt, and old sneakers. It was now that I discovered the holes and tears that littered my clothing, giving me a homeless appearance. Why would I expect anyone to open the door and allow me into their house looking such a mess?

Zeke, on the other hand, was well put together. He looked to be about 6'3" and was dressed in dark jeans and a green button down. He had short brunette hair that matched his brown eyes and dark complexion. The only seemingly out of place quality was a burn scar on his forearm.

Neither of us sat. Either we were both equally as nervous, or he didn't want a complete stranger sitting on his pristine white couches. Whatever the case, I preferred pacing.

"Start talking." He said in between sips of water.

"Okay, I don't know how else to say this, so I'm just going to blurt it all out. Basically, we were both operated on by Mandala. I know this because my mother and uncle used to work there. But recently, my mother was murdered by them, and it was made to look like a suicide. I found your picture in a photo album, and I'd like your help at hunting them down and stopping them." I just blurted everything out as best I could. At that moment, Zeke sat down. He put a hand to his head as if to stop a migraine.

"Where is your dad?" He asked with a confused look.

I was just as confused by his question. "Dead," I responded.

And then I realized why he was asking.

"Where are your parents?" I asked, trying to fit the puzzle pieces.

"Died in gas station explosion four years ago." He responded, with an all too familiar tone.

At that moment, is when *I* finally sat down. The realization hit me.

Mandala was killing off our parents.

Chapter 5
Zeke

It was a weekend afternoon. To Zeke and his family, it meant a trip to watch their favorite baseball team in Jacksonville. The whole family made their way into their dad's F-150, all dressed in baseball jerseys and wearing baseball caps. Zeke's dad was in the driver's seat, and his mom was riding shotgun, while Zeke and his sister had the back seat to themselves.

Their dad's love for baseball had been contagious. Zeke himself had played baseball up until high school but was not good enough to make it to his college's team. However, that did not dampen his love for the game. He even volunteered to coach middle school students at the community fields during the week. They never missed a baseball game, and this game, in particular, had Zeke's dad pumped. The team's rivals were in town, and they needed the win badly to keep up the chances of winning the league.

As they rode through town on the way to the game, Zeke's dad turned on the radio to listen to the pre-game analysis. The sports analyst shared the same views as Zeke's dad about which player should bat first.

"Hey guys I need to get gas. Anyone want some snacks?" Zeke's dad asked as he turned into the gas station.

"Yeah, can I get a soda and some chips? Not the regular ones though, the ones with onions and pepper."

"Eeew! I wonder why you like that stuff anyway." His sister Tiffany exclaimed with a look of disgust on her face.

"How 'bout you miss? Want anything?" Zeke's dad asked with laughter at his kids.

"No, I'm good," Tiffany answered.

"I'm not sure I know the sort of chips you want, but I'll get you one." Zeke's dad said as he got down from the truck.

"You know what? I think I'll just get it myself." Zeke said, getting down from the truck and headed for the mart while his dad pumped gas. Zeke walked out of the mart hugging two cans of chips under one arm, while he drank from the soda in his other hand. As he got closer to the gas pump where his dad's truck was parked, he noticed a man dressed in the opposing teams' jersey walking away from his dad's truck. Zeke's dad yelled at him as the man made for his bike that was some distance away. From a distance, it seemed the man must have said or done something to upset Zeke's dad.

The man got on his bike, and before he zoomed off, he rolled a baseball in the direction of the truck. The object stopped just under the bed of the truck. Zeke looked in his dad's direction. He could tell his dad was confused as he glanced from the truck to the seemingly crazy guy that was now joining the freeway. Zeke was walking toward the truck with a mind to ask his dad what that was about when he was suddenly thrown forcefully by a loud bang.

The snacks he had purchased went flying in all directions. It had all happened so fast, he didn't have time to process what was going on. Lying on the floor and unable to hear anything over the loud ringing in his ears, the last thing he saw was his dad's truck engulfed in flames.

***

"A huge gas explosion left three dead and one critically injured this evening at a gas station," the horrific news report was displayed on the TV in the hospital room Zeke was being held in. "It has been reported that it was a malfunction with the gas pump..."

Zeke faded in and out of consciousness, still unsure of the events that unfolded in front of him. His thoughts were jumbled with vivid images of fierce flames and piercing screams ripping through his ears. The screams caused his ears to ring, or was it the fire? Zeke wasn't sure of anything anymore, and being all alone in the isolated white room made everything even more uncertain. Nothing could have prepared him or his family for the explosion.

Nothing could have prepared him for a goodbye or an "I love you". Zeke closed his eyes attempting to force himself into an inevitable slumber. He didn't want to be awake, and he never wanted to wake up. His body ached; all the while his face soaked with silent tears, wishing for it all to be a terrible nightmare. Maybe it was a nightmare? Zeke considered himself a decent person. He never set out to harm others, so why was his life taking a turn for the worst? All the questions flooding his mind gave him a sharp headache. Was this his reality now? As an orphan? His parents and younger sister were dead, all because of a stupid gas station. He was only 21 years old. He was supposed to watch his sister get married, watch his parents get old together, and live a fantastic life. But now he had no one. He was alone. Even though he was an adult, he felt like a vulnerable child needing guidance on what to do next.

His emotions were a mixture of sadness and overwhelming hatred. That gas station was going to pay. He was going to ruin their lives the way they did his. How was it that he managed to escape the explosion with a headache and a few small burns, while the rest of his family burned to an agonizing death?

His heart condition was acting up more so than ever before. His chest felt tight, and he couldn't tell if he was having a heart attack or not. Zeke's breathing hitched, and he desperately tried to reach over for the nurse's button. Zeke had no way to control his stress. It was a recipe for disaster for anyone with congestive heart disease. "Heart attack at 21. It's a shame." A physician was speaking to his medical scribe while assessing Zeke when he noticed he had awakened.

"How are you feeling, bud?" He questioned.

Zeke gave him a slight nod but was also recovering from the shock of having had a heart attack. Too much was going on now. Having a heart attack at such a young age increases the risk of death at an early age by an exceptional percentage. These circumstances were reducing any willpower left in order to defeat another severe heart malfunction.

Within a few days, Zeke was released from the hospital and back to his now empty, hollow household. Anger consumed his every thought and prevented him from continuing his old life. He got into contact with the family lawyer and immediately binged on a lawsuit against the gas station that destroyed his family. The gas station had argued that a secondary reason had caused the explosion, but the forensics investigators could not find anything to prove it.

In the end, it took him nearly a year learning all of the ins and outs about the relevant law and eventually, winning the case with minimal help from his useless lawyer. The money could not fill the gaping hole in his heart. He initially splurged on liquor, girls, shopping, and more liquor; but he had to put an end to it as his heart condition got worse from his reckless life. He desperately sought for anything that would distract him from his thoughts and take the constant pain away. This phase fizzled out quickly upon the realization of the inevitable. He could not be happy. Not while his blood was dead but not avenged.

Chapter 6
Zoe

Following our sudden realization that Mandala was murdering our parents, Zeke allowed James into the house and explained what had happened to him. I was devastated for him and how much he had lost. None of this was right, and we needed to do something about it.

We brought Zeke up to speed and told him what our plan was; to find Zoe and Amy for more helping hands and insight. Since Zeke was fairly wealthy and had no reason to keep a steady job except to keep his mind busy, he reluctantly agreed and began packing a bag. Now was a time where he could finally do more about what happened to his family.

Zeke was kind, given everything he had gone through. There was a flicker of anger in his eyes, but it was always overcome by warmth when he'd speak to us. I couldn't imagine living alone in such a big house that I had once shared with a family. Maybe, that's partly why he'd been so willing to join us. Loneliness? Relief? Finally, answers?

While he packed, he allowed us to shower in his home and raid his refrigerator. We were starved and more than happy that our newest acquaintance had money to feed our appetites. A long car ride awaited us, and I just hoped that the same conversation with Zoe would go just as smoothly as it did with Zeke.

He seemed smart and was able to understand the severity of the situation quickly. Once we were finally settled in for the drive, I explained that our next visit was to Zoe Knight, a 27-year-old with leukemia. We all let out an exasperated sigh at the mention of another illness. Just the thought of receiving these fatal illnesses and diseases at such young ages intentionally was unsettling.

We had about a day's drive ahead of us, and for some reason, I found myself in the back seat of my own car. I decided to take advantage and stretched myself out for a much-needed nap. Unfortunately, about an hour later, I was rudely awoken to the sound of the Firebird getting rear-ended. My body hit the seats in front of me, and I jolted awake.

"Please do not tell me that was what I think it was." I groaned.

As soon as I turned to look through the back windshield, the car that hit us appeared to be making a run for it. While I screamed profanity from the inside of the car, I caught a glimpse of strawberry blonde hair.

"You've got to be kidding me," I mumbled.

It was Felicity.

Given the situation, I needed to fess up to James and Zeke about this so-called "friend" I made. While I explained the story, I slowly realized how big of an idiot I was, and James made sure to let me know.

"You decide to speak to strangers *now*?" He yelled.

"I'm sorry! It seemed harmless!" I attempted to defend myself feebly but knew I messed up big time. I would probably never hear the end of this. While Zeke tried his best to mediate between us, we realized a more significant problem was now at hand. Even Zeke did not know what our next step for getting help would be. If Felicity is somehow connected to this whole situation, who's to say she isn't on her way to Zoe right now? With that in mind, James put the car in drive, and we were off, burning fuel faster than ever before. This suddenly felt like a race, and the minutes seemed to be flying by. What I expected to be a scenic road trip filled with waffles from diners turned into a greasy drive-thru for the sake of making it to Zoe on time. We stopped for the bathroom only when we needed to fill gas and never complained about needing to stretch our legs. We all knew what the stakes were.

With how fast we were driving, I tried to slow down the time by boring holes into the passing mountains with my eyes. I loved mountains and wished I could have been visiting North Carolina in better circumstances. I tried to imagine how Zoe would be. For making it to be 27 years old, she must have gone into remission, right? I pictured her as an interior designer or a chef. Maybe she lived in a cabin in the mountains?

Hopefully, a much nicer cabin than James' hideout. My mind got away from me as I came up with all of these hypothetical scenarios with some form of hope in this horrible mess. I imagined myself waltzing into her cabin with her at the front, expecting me all along. She would be ready to help immediately and easily drop everything just as Zeke had. But first, she would cook us a four-course meal given that she was a fantastic chef, and we would bond over our love for Italian food while we sipped on old wine. She would pack extra clothes to share with me, and we would become the best of friends on our way to Amy. I played this entire fantasy in my head over and over again until we reached her apartment in the city. Zeke had increased my expectations. If Zoe is alive, she could offer us more help as willingly as he did. Apartment in the city. From the start, this was not going to play out anything like my fantasy.

There was no cabin in the mountains. I didn't smell pasta being made. I didn't waltz into her home, and she wasn't ready to help. Instead, we broke into her apartment on the fourth floor and smelled a decaying body. I fell to my knees with Zeke's hands on my shoulders.

"No, no, no, no!" I crumpled my fists while tears rolled down my cheeks. "She can't be dead, she can't be dead, she can't be dead!" I looked up to James, hopeless, not knowing what to do. Tears welled up in my eyes, and my head suddenly weighed a thousand pounds. I so badly wanted to destroy what was left of the company that experimented on me. That experimented with all of us. Zoe looked peaceful. I couldn't comprehend her death at all. It couldn't have been Felicity. Given the smell, she had obviously been in here rotting. Was it the cancer? Was she killed? All I knew was that these questions had to wait. We were running out of time. We quickly called 911 and pretended to be renters informing them that we smelled something awful. While we rummaged through the paperwork on her desk, we discovered that she did know about Mandala and was beginning to do her own research.

She had the same list of names that I had and had also crossed off everyone that was deceased. My heart ached while grabbing all the paperwork and pictures. Her handwriting seemed shaky and rushed. We hurried out of the apartment with our shirts covering our mouths and noses. Once we made it outside, Zeke ran over to some bushes to vomit.

The smell was not pleasant, and I wasn't sure how we would ever be able to erase it from our memories. Although I'm sure he was strong, such a situation was enough to break down anyone. I finally assessed the damage to my car from Felicity's hit and run and only saw a small scratch. "She got lucky," I thought to myself. I dug through the bags of chips in the backseat with an empty appetite.

"What are we supposed to do now?" I asked.

"We keep going," James said. And with that, we were off yet again with an even greater journey ahead of us. I looked at Zeke for a while, trying to read his mind. We had just dumped all of this information on him and led him straight to a corpse. Did he want to back out? Did he think we were insane? I just wanted to know what was going through his head.

His head was leaned against the window with his eyes closed, but I knew he wasn't asleep. None of us would be sleeping for a while after that ordeal. Zeke had behaved ideally to this point. Perhaps the loss of his family had hardened his resolve considerably. Like me, he wouldn't be happy until he held the company responsible for their atrocities.

"Alice," a murmur came from Zeke.

"Yeah?" I responded.

"I can feel your eyes," Zeke complained.

"Oh, sorry." I let out an embarrassed chuckle.

Zeke assured me that he was fine and just overwhelmed. After a serious talk about making sure that he was capable of handling the Firebird, he and James switched places so that James could nap for a while. I continued to shove my fists into a flaming hot Cheetos bag nervously and after a few hours, begged Zeke to stop for coffee. James refused to get up from his nap, and given our recent loss of motivation, Zeke and I decided to get out and stretch our legs at a coffee shop in the middle of nowhere. We ordered and sat at a table near a window so we could keep an eye on James and the car. I was more concerned about the car.

"So, what are the chances that "Amy with Alzheimer's" is our savior?" Zeke sighed exhaustedly.

I laughed painfully at the nickname and reminded him that he had a heart attack at just 21 years of age. For his troubles, he sure offered me comic relief. While we sat there, silently sipping our coffee and taking occasional glances toward James, I had a sudden realization.

"I can track Felicity!" I blurted. Zeke looked at me with curiosity but evident confusion, and I explained to him that I had a technological genius friend back home who could easily track Felicity's phone since I had her number. I phoned my goofy friend, Finn, who had worked with me at the bowling alley for a painful number of years.

"Alice, is that really you?" he stammered from the other end of the line. "Yeah, it's me, Finn." I realized I had avoided so many people since my mother died that I really hadn't had a chance to explain myself. Finn was my right hand, and I was suddenly feeling like the biggest jerk in the world for leaving him out of everything.

I briefly explained to him that I was trying to find out more about my mother's death and that it had led me out of state. I didn't want to give him too many details, but I needed to provide him with enough information to ensure that he would help. I explained to him that there was a super sketchy lady I met at a library that somehow followed me to North Carolina and that I had her phone number and needed for him to work his magic.

"Say no more."

I texted him her cell phone number, and he hung up and assured me he'd work as fast as possible.

Not even five minutes had passed when I received a phone call from him.

"Alice, where is your exact location right now?"

I told him we were at a diner called Dixie's Diner.

"Felicity is 500 feet from you!" he yelled into the phone so loud that Zeke could hear.

We immediately bolted to the Firebird, nearly giving James a heart attack.

"James, we gotta go. Felicity is literally on top of us!" I yelled while Zeke started the car.

I forgot that I had left Finn on the phone until I heard him screaming through the other end.

"She's getting closer to you!" He yelled as we practically drove in circles, not knowing where to go.

Her black SUV finally appeared behind us while we screamed nonsense.

"Alice! Get behind her car, I have an idea!" Finn was now on speaker trying to help.

Zeke did some impressive maneuvering and finally placed us behind her car on a one-way road with plenty of traffic coming from the opposite direction. She couldn't go anywhere now.

"Read me her license plate," Finn demanded. We were still confused as to how this was helpful but did as we were told. As soon as we read the license plate, Finn hung up.

"What the hell, Finn?" I yelled in frustration. We could see Felicity turning around occasionally to make sure we were still tailing her. I didn't know what our next move was. Should we turn off the road? Put as much distance between us as possible? But now she was ahead of us, and we needed to make it to Amy before her. I was lost. Clearly, I had no plan or idea left to execute. My phone started ringing, and I saw Finn's goofy face pop up on the screen. I immediately answered and suddenly saw the colors of the American flag flashing behind us.

James and Zeke noticed as well, and we all stopped screaming and sat calmly.

"Finn. What the hell do we do now?" I seethed through my teeth as if somehow the cop behind us could hear me.

"Listen to me carefully. In 800 feet, turn onto Harrow Hill drive on your right." He stayed on the phone while we made the turn expecting the police vehicle to follow us.

Instead, the cop went gunning for Felicity in her black SUV. Relieved, we all let out a sigh.

"Finn, I love you!" I exclaimed through the phone.

"She shouldn't be a problem anymore," he stated. "If you need more help, I'll be on standby." I decided to take his offer more seriously to give myself some security in taking down Mandala. I sent Finn a text. "I'm emailing you a file that I need you to put on a flash drive. If anything is to happen to me, I want you to release it to all news sources." It was a file I had taken the time to compile during my time at the library. It contained pictures, names, and dates of all of the babies that were experimented on, along with any other incriminating evidence I could piece together. If, for some reason, none of this was to work out, I needed to ensure that the company would be dismembered or at least exposed.

Chapter 7
Amy

Once we gathered ourselves after the intense high-speed chase, we refocused on the importance of reaching Amy before the company did. I was anxious and flustered. If Amy were another dead end, I wouldn't know what to do. I needed more estrogen in the temper-filled car, and I needed to hold onto hope somehow. With each name I had to cross off the list, I felt a little emptier inside.

Even though I never truly knew these people, we had been through a major event together, and that had to mean something. I wanted my research and the road trip to pay off in the end. I wanted this entire adventure to have meaning and to bring vengeance for my mom, to have vengeance for me.

It had been years, and if Mandala was still around murdering people from its past, there had to be something new going on. This idea brought me much worry. What if other babies were being brought into the labs? Had our failure not proven the worthlessness of what the company was experimenting with? I was biting my nails again without even realizing it. James gave me a look through the rearview mirror to stop. He always yelled at me when I was younger for nail-biting. I folded my hands in my lap with the embarrassment a ten-year-old would feel. Did five missing years really make our relationship this strange?

"Nervous?" Zeke asked after catching sight of my furrowed brows.

I couldn't even pretend to be brave at this point. So many things could go wrong. "I really hope she's in there."

Zeke shrugged his shoulders. He was still skeptical. Even if she was alive, she still had Alzheimer's, and what help would that be in this matter? I knew he was right to be wary, but we had nothing else to hold onto. Our road trip continued with no other complications, and we made it safely to New Jersey.

"Are we there yet?" I annoyed James with my childish questions to make the time go by. "Five minutes," his response struck us with anticipation, and we immediately felt more awake. The road trip had definitely drained us all, and we could only hope that it had been worth it.

*****

The three of us slowly made our way toward what was supposed to be Amy's house. The building was similar to most farmhouses, it was surrounded by a picket fence that had lost its white hue, and from where we stood, we could make out a couple of barns that must have been used as storage for whatever produce was being farmed at the time.

We had left the Firebird some distance away, not wanting to spook Amy unnecessarily, knowing her condition. It would have been challenging if she had a breakdown while we were approaching her. I could tell from the look on James and Zeke's faces that no one wanted a repeat of what they had experienced at Zoe's place, myself included.

Another dead person would have hindered our resolve in following through with the plan. Expectantly, we moved forward and approached Amy's house. James was the first to climb the steps that led to the porch, while Zeke and I followed closely, looking around for any unusual signs. The house seemed to be in the middle of nowhere, meaning we were far from any possible help, which aided the cause of the evil company we were up against. James raised the knocker on the door and gave the door two firm knocks. We waited for what seemed to be forever. He knocked again, but there was no response from inside the house. No sound of movement could be heard. This was not the most favorable result for us, especially after the previous experience at Zoe's home.

"I don't think anyone is home," Zeke said, voicing out the exact thoughts of the rest of us. It seemed like we were going to have to make a forced entry again. Zeke walked to the nearest window and tried to move it from the outside, but it did not budge. We went around the house together, looking for a window that may have been left open.

"We'll check the barns when we are done here," James said as he tried another window. As soon as James finished his statement, the window gave a shrill sound as it moved.

"Finally."

"Alice, you're the only one that can fit. Crawl through and open the front door for us. Don't go looking around yet," James warned. "Okay," I answered. My heart began to race, realizing I was about to go in on my own. I hoped a similar sight like Zoe's would not greet me. I knew I just didn't have it in me to see one more failure.

"Be careful," James called out from behind me as I climbed into the window. Zeke had provided me with a boost with his palms and knees, so I did not have to jump for the edge of the window. I gave the guys a thumbs-up sign as soon as I was in. I was standing in a rather large kitchen. There was no putrid smell from anywhere, which I was thankful for.

Amy had probably moved away, I thought. The house felt empty and unused. Although her absence did not help in any way, it was still better than finding her dead and rotting. I made my way from the kitchen, past a dining room and a couple of locked doors, and went straight to the front door just like James had instructed. The sitting room was somewhat dark as most of the blinds were drawn, but there was still enough light for me to make my way to the front door. The door was covered in various locks and bolts that I unchained and turned. I finally made my way to the doorknob, which would not budge.

"James! James!" I called out beyond the door.

"Yes. What's happening?"

"There's no key in the lock. I unbolted everything else." I said, looking around the sitting room at the same time, hoping to find a key rack. But it was a futile effort in the low light.

"You have to look around. Check for any drawers or cabinets," James called from behind the door.

I was flustered and getting more panicked by the second. The farmhouse was huge and overwhelming, and I had no clue as to where the key could be hiding.

Minutes went by as I rummaged through different drawers but to no success.

Zeke proved to be especially impatient because, with no warning, the door was kicked in.

I jumped, stunned from their burst through the door.

"I guess that makes you an expert at breaking and entering," a small voice said from behind me.

I froze in my position, and the voice came again.

"Move it. All of you." I moved out of the way to reveal a female pointing a shotgun in our direction.

Seeing the gun pointed at us made my mind start racing. I had a million questions, but the one that kept on repeating itself in my head was, is she with Mandala? "Who are you?" Zeke asked in a quivering voice. It seemed he was the most courageous of us. I imagined how his heart was holding up, given the situation we were in. It would be quite disastrous for him to have a heart attack right now.

"Shut up. I'll be asking all the questions." The lady said in her tiny voice while trying her best to sound intimidating. Apart from the gun that she was holding, nothing was intimidating about her. She was slightly taller than I was, and in the low light, I could tell she had blonde hair; she was the sort of girl that made the captain of the cheerleading team. But this cheerleader had a gun in place of pom-poms. She waved us over into the sitting room and gestured for us to sit with her shotgun.

"Who are you? And why did you break into my house?" I let out a silent sigh of relief when she qualified the house as hers. For a while, I was beginning to fear we had fallen into the custody of a member of Mandala.

"We're sorry for breaking into your house. You must be Amy." James said while standing from his seat to offer her a hand. "Sit down! And how do you know my name?" She said, now sounding more confident than before.

"We've come a long way to find you. We don't mean you any harm, and I suggest you drop the gun. There's no need for it." James was doing his best to speak in a fatherly and comforting tone, but it wasn't working on this stubborn blonde.

"You don't get to tell me what to do. You've come a long way, yeah? From where? What do you want?"

"We-we." James began to stutter, and he was starting to sound very unsure of himself.

"Amy, we mean you no harm. In fact, we are just as scared as you are." I jumped in, trying to save the situation.

"Who says I'm scared," Amy said with a scornful smile at the corner of her lips.

"I guess you're trying to protect yourself from Mandala. The same company that gave you Alzheimer's." I delivered it as direct as I could. Amy dropped the gun to her side all of a sudden.

"How do you know that? How do you know about Mandala?" Realizing she had not received a convincing answer, she raised the gun and pointed it at us again.

"Do you work for Mandala?" Amy bellowed.

Deep down, I was praying Amy did not have a breakdown while still holding onto the gun. As confident as she seemed, I noticed her hands began to shake.

"We don't work for Mandala. We are victims of Mandala just like you." I said as I shifted uneasily on the sofa.

"Yes. We are!" Zeke added after an eternity of silence from him.

"You all have been experimented on?"

"Yes." Zeke and I chorused.

Amy turned to look at James, noticing he did not answer her question. "What about you? Were you experimented on?"

"No, but Mandala killed my sister while trying to keep their activities a secret," he responded somberly as if it were a sentence he was tired of repeating. Explaining that

James used to work for Mandala would probably not help in our current situation. He glanced at me with a nod, as if he was saying, "We'll tell her later, preferably not with a shotgun pointed at us."

"OK. I get it now. You guys have a history with Mandala, but I don't still understand what you're doing here, in my house." Amy was going to be difficult, which was apparent. She was more stubborn than I was, which says a lot.

"We came to offer you help," Zeke said. His nerves had dissipated, and now he just sounded annoyed. Zeke had been the least excited to find Amy, and I quickly gave him a nudge to hide his attitude.

"As you can see, I can handle myself adequately," Amy said while waving the gun.

"Yeah, I guess you can. But you can't go on living like this forever, always watching your back, and not knowing who is coming for you." I forgave Zeke's arguing tone since he was speaking the truth.

"I don't have a choice. It's the only way I know how to survive." Amy's words struck me. Finding her, Zoe, and

Zeke truly made me realize the after-effects of Mandala's experiments. People like Amy and Zoe had known about the antics for longer than I did. I wondered how it had affected them to live in constant fear, whereas I had remained oblivious for the better part of my life. The effects were life-changing, both physically and mentally; and Amy had to learn how to survive on her own, with Alzheimer's.

The closer I looked in the light, I saw that her house was covered in colorful sticky notes that reminded her of basic things in life. "Your bedroom is upstairs," one read. "The bathroom is down the hall, to the right," another informed. Amy walked over to the center coffee table and placed the gun down. Seeing her drop the gun produced a sigh of relief from each of us. She must have realized we were of no threat to her. Her gesture had eased the tension in the room considerably. James stood up from his seat and walked over to her. "Well, we could bring it to a stop."

"How do you plan on doing that?" Amy asked with a quizzical look on her face. "We're going to bring Mandala down," James said as he placed a hand on Amy's shoulder in a reassuring manner. Amy burst out in hysterical laughter. Her outburst caused a bit of panic as we looked at each other clueless, wondering what was going on.

"Sorry-sorry. What did you just say? You're going to take down Mandala?" She said while still trying to suppress her laughter.

"Yes. We are." I snapped. Her disbelief was beginning to irritate me, or maybe it was a result of all the anger I had bottled up inside me. I could not imagine how she could be comfortable knowing someone was out there responsible for her ailment. Her outburst made me feel childish. As determined as I was, was I ignorant enough to believe that this would be a possible feat? Her doubt caused me to rethink everything.

"You and what army?" Amy asked with an apparent look of defiance. It made me wonder whether we were dealing with this issue in the right way. Amy was like a ticking time bomb.

"Us. We came for your help too." James said. I could tell that he was thinking things over too. "I like your confidence, but you just told me they killed your sister. They won't bat an eyelash to kill any other person." We knew this was true, but the idea of vengeance outweighed the possible risks.

"We know the odds are against us, but we have nothing left to lose," Zeke said before pausing for a brief second. "My mom, dad, and sister died in a gas station explosion. It all seemed like a freak accident at first, I even sued the gas station, but something didn't add up. A man at the gas station rolled a baseball under my dad's truck before the accident. In retrospect, I'm sure it must have been some kind of explosive, and the man must have been working with Mandala." Zeke's gaze hit the floor. He couldn't make eye contact with any of us while thinking about what happened to his family.

"Well, they did not have a problem killing my dad either. And he was a trained soldier. He taught me everything I know. But still, he wasn't a match for them. So instead of facing them, I think I'd rather hide." Amy hid her emotions and only spoke with doubt. She was doing the math in her head and preferred to risk staying alone. As strong and as tough as she was, she knew her chances.

"They killed your dad?" I asked in disbelief as if I was unaware of the atrocities they were capable of. Every single one of us seemed to be an orphan. Mandala was leaving no clues behind for anyone to catch on to them.

"Yes, they did. When I turned eighteen, my dad explained to me how I had gotten Alzheimer's. He told me how they had no idea it was going to turn that way, and that they were just taking me to run some tests for a research trial. When he found out, he threatened them legally, but they had connections. They made all of the relevant evidence disappear. After ruining his legal base, they got physical. He told me how we had to abandon our home and came to stay at my grandparent's house.

They eventually killed him when he traveled to North Carolina to get some evidence on Mandala. He had researched new evidence that had the potential of putting them down for good, so they found and killed him. Ever since he died, I've been in hiding. I rarely leave the house, and I'm wary of strangers. So, when I saw you guys, I thought you were one of them." Amy took a seat, confirming her newfound trust.

"I'm sorry to hear that, but if we were able to find you so easily, they could find you too," James pointed out.

"Correction, you did not find me. I found you."

"If you had thought we worked for Mandala, why didn't you open fire then?" Zeke asked.

"You guys didn't seem like some mean killers, you looked lost. I had to confirm, and my curiosity got the better of me," she admitted.

"Do you think you'll join us? We always need to stay ahead of Mandala." We were wasting time getting to know each other, and I was in a hurry.

"No, I don't think so. As I said, I can handle myself." Frustration was building inside of me. How could she not understand how big this was? Hadn't she done her research on Mandala as well? I didn't know why she wasn't as willing as myself and Zeke.

"Let me show you something," I pulled out the picture I had used in tracking down Zeke as well as Amy.

"What's this?" Amy asked as she walked over to my side.

James pulled back the curtains to bring more light into the room.

"What am I looking at? Why are some faces crossed out?" Amy inquired impatiently.

"It's a picture of some of the kids Mandala experimented on. There might be more, we aren't certain yet. But every other person in the picture apart from us are all dead. That's why their faces are crossed out. We have to do this for all of them."

"Hell, this is bigger than I thought." Amy gasped and brought a hand to her heart.

"You're right. It's bigger than you thought. There's no telling how many more people they have killed in order to cover up their operations. But apart from that, they are unremorsefully endangering people's lives with their experiments. Zeke has a heart condition, Alice has congenital insensitivity to pain, and you have Alzheimer's, as a result of their experiments.

They need to be held accountable for their actions. The rest of the world needs to know what they did." James said in a gruff voice. I could hear the emotion behind his words, and the regret he must've felt. It was obvious he felt some sense of responsibility for all of the deaths that had happened. Amy shook her head as she took in the new information.

"I need to take my medications, give me a minute," Amy informed the group, then walked out of the sitting room and down the same corridor I had come from. Her footsteps were audible as she climbed the stairs.

"What do you think?" I asked as soon as I was sure she was out of earshot.

"I think she's okay. But we need to leave soon, with or without her." James said.

"You can't be seriously thinking of leaving without her," Zeke added.

"It's her decision to follow us or not. We can't force her into coming along." James seemed conflicted. I could tell he didn't like having to convince her to join us. It brought back too many memories for him to want to explain again. I could tell he wanted to avoid Amy asking more questions.

"That's true. But as stubborn as she is, I think it would be good to have her along. She seems like a tough one." I said as I glanced in the direction of the gun.

"Can we at least spend the night here? I'm tired of sleeping in the car." Zeke complained, prompting an annoyed glance from me as if he had insulted the Firebird. He was right, though. My limbs felt stiff and sore, as well. The idea of a bed appealed to me immensely. "We can talk that over when Amy gets back. There's a lot we still need to discuss before we set out. She obviously knows about Mandala, and we'll need every bit of information she has about their current status."

Although James had acquired a considerable amount of knowledge while working at Mandala, Amy was better informed on their more recent events, especially with her father's research. It was imperative to get every ounce of knowledge on Mandala that we could.

Chapter 8
The Plan

The light streaking in through the window blinds served as my wake up call. Although I had trouble falling asleep in an unfamiliar bed, I was thankful for a proper night's rest. After much deliberation on the previous day, we had agreed to slow things down a bit to get a definite plan of action.

Amy was quite particular about that. She had decided to join us only if we went over the plan to bring down Mandala with her. As of yesterday, it was obvious we did not have a plan set in place. We were just winging it up until that point. Our knowledge of Mandala was mostly vague, and the little information we had was all from James, which according to him had a fair chance of being obsolete.

After reviewing the knowledge James and Amy had, we all sat together and went over the notes from Zoe's apartment. Amy suggested we infiltrate Mandala and disable whatever security protocol they had from the inside. At first, it sounded like a pipe dream. We did not have the knowledge to disable security systems. Then James remembered my friend Finn and proposed a scenario where Finn could be of help. I called Finn, and he assured me it was no problem if we could get a flash drive; he would send us an intrusive malware over the internet, and we could download it onto the flash drive.

All we needed to do was plug it into any of their systems, and he'd take it from there. So, we were set to take down Mandala, we just had to get a flash drive and a wireless earpiece for communication with Finn, once we were inside the facility. As I was still going through the plan in my head, I heard a knock on my door and Amy walked in without waiting for a reply.

"Hey there, slept well?" Amy asked with a smile on her face.

"Yeah, I did. Thanks."

"Good. I'm about to fix some breakfast, and we'll be ready to hit the road in no time."

"Sounds great. I'll be out soon," I said while stretching my arms.

"Alright."

I got out of bed and headed for the bathroom. The bedroom was spacious and had a bath and toilet attached. According to Amy, the house belonged to her maternal grandfather, who used to train horses. It was then passed on to her parents. Her mom married a soldier, and they had lived together here. Amy's mom had died when she was 12 during the birth of her second child. Now she was an orphan, thanks to Mandala.

I quickly showered myself and tried to take in every second of the hot water. The long road trip had made me feel incredibly dirty, and I was happy to have someone close to my size that I could borrow clothes from. During breakfast, I couldn't help but feel enthusiastic and positive. We were finally making headway, and I was glad to have successfully found Amy.

"It's good to see you smiling again," James interjected between bites of his bread. Apparently, my mood was quite obvious. "Maybe, I just can't wait to get on the road again," I said trying to hide my expressions. I did not want to give James a feeling that I had forgiven him for his actions. Although he claimed it was in our interest, the fact that he had left still hurt me, and I was still trying to bring myself to the realization that our lives would never be the same again. Zeke and Amy ate on in silence, probably contemplating the journey ahead and its dangers.

"We should be leaving in the next hour," James said as he pushed back his seat. I finished the rest of my breakfast and headed to the kitchen to help tidy up. By the time we finished cleaning up, we were almost ready to go.

"Amy, are you done packing?' James called to her from the kitchen entrance.

"Yeah!" Amy answered as she made her way downstairs.

"I just need to pack some extra shotgun shells."

James gave her a questioning look, most likely remembering that she could serve as a danger at any second, given her condition.

"I know what you're thinking, but I haven't had an episode in two years," Amy stated as a matter of fact, as she continued shoving shotgun shells in her bag. She read his mind. "OK then. Are we all ready?" James said as he glanced from one face to the other.

Zeke and I gave him a brisk nod.

"Amy, finish packing the shells and meet us outside. Remember to pack light."

The three of us headed out of the broken front door that Zeke had busted through barely twenty-four hours ago. Somehow, it felt like longer than that. I was the last to head out of the house, and linger for a brief second before attempting to shut the broken door behind me.

We walked the distance to the picket fence and waited for Amy there. After a few minutes, she made her way to us, coming out of the back door. It seemed she did not like using the front entrance.

"Where to now?" Amy asked as she joined us. She had a green duffel bag with her and looked like she was setting out for an adventure.

"We'll head for the Firebird now. From there to a store where we can get what we need," James informed her.

We all walked briskly to where the Firebird was parked. James had made sure to conceal it properly from sight. Even if someone else had come along, they were sure to miss it. I guess all those years when he was on the run had taught him quite a number of things about avoiding others. Perhaps, he learned something when avoiding Mom and me.

James got behind the wheel, and I got into the passenger seat as Amy and Zeke climbed into the back seat. He turned the key in the ignition, and the Firebird roared to life. In no time, we were back on the freeway and in search of a store to purchase the flash drive that we would need for Finn's malware.

We passed by other cars, and it occurred to me that the passing faces were utterly oblivious to our world and what was going on in it. Even if they did, I wondered if they would care to do anything about it. From the little experience I had with people, they always tended to avoid dealing with other people's issues. James pulled up into a parking lot, and his voice snapped me out of my thoughts.

"I think Zeke and Amy should wait behind while we get what we need. Do you guys want anything?"

"We're good," Amy answered for the duo.

Zeke just gazed on in silence and nodded in agreement.

I got out of the car and joined James at the entrance to the store. It was a small electronic shop that sold gadgets and accessories for cheaper than a major retailer.

James walked straight to the attendant and requested a flash drive and a wireless earpiece. He wasn't interested in chatting about the available brands. He only cared for a flash drive with the largest memory storage and an earpiece that worked. We quickly paid for it and just as we were about to leave, he turned back to ask, "Where could I get a laptop?"

"What kind of PC do you need? We've got both new ones and refurbished ones." The plump attendant asked.

"I'm not looking to buy one, I need one I could use just for about thirty minutes."

"Oh! OK. There's a library not too far from here. They have computers that you could use on a time basis."

"Thanks," James said while giving the attendant a nod. We headed out and got back into the car. As we drove out of the parking lot, I got out my phone and dialed Finn.

"Hey, Finn." I said into the phone as I watched out for any library as James drove along.

"We've got the flash now, we're headed to use a PC at a library." Finn dictated to me an address to a cloud account. All I had to do was log into the account and download the file.

"Hey look, there's the library," I exclaimed as I pointed in the direction of an old public library marquee.

As we pulled into the library's parking lot, the weather was beginning to turn gloomy.

"We've got to be quick about this, the weather's changing. I don't want to be caught in a storm while driving." James said.

"OK. Got it." I replied as I grabbed the flash from the Firebird's glove compartment with one hand and opened the door with the other.

"How long is it going to take?" James asked.

"Finn said it'll take about ten minutes to download, but might take longer depending on the connection speed," I informed him.

"Do you need me to come along?"

"No, I'm fine." James had become more and more overbearing throughout the trip. I felt like I was a kid again.

"OK, but if you're not out in twenty minutes, I'll come to check up on you."

"Fine. Let's hope I don't have to stay that long." I replied as I shut the car door.

I walked to the entrance of the library. It was a small building made of red bricks. I hoped I wouldn't have to explain myself to anyone this time around, as I walked into the library. By now, I knew better than just blabbing to a complete stranger. At the entrance, there was a sign that showed directions to the reading room and the computer section.

I followed the arrow to the right and pushed open a glass door to a completely deserted computer section besides a man in his late 30's. He was typing away on the keyboard as I entered and did not seem to pay me any attention. I picked a seat at the end of the row where he was seated. If he wanted to have any conversation, he'd have to get up from his seat and walk over; something I very much doubted he'll want to do, but I took the precaution all the same.

I pulled out my phone and looked at the address Finn had given me. I felt grateful to have him as one of my loyal friends. I pulled out the keyboard tray and punched in the address. A red and white window popped up on the browser and asked me to enter in my login details.

I glanced back at my phone before inputting the username and password. Just like Finn had explained, it took me to another window where there was the option of downloading the file. I quickly plugged in the flash drive and began to download it. Finn had estimated about ten minutes for the download, and it only took seven. As soon as I was done, I pulled out the flash drive and headed for the exit.

The man was still typing away on his keyboard, but as I passed him on my way out, he turned to look at me and smiled. His smile was unnerving, like he knew something I didn't. It got me thinking till I got to the car. I hoped he was not somehow working with Mandala. Although it seemed far off, I had come to believe Mandala was entirely capable of anything.

"Are you done?" James asked as I got into the car.

"Yeah, I'm done. We can go now." My face was stone cold. I felt like I was overthinking every interaction now and wasn't sure if I should tell him about my encounter.

"What's the matter? Did anyone bother you while you were inside?"

James was still quite capable of reading my emotions, and I had forgotten all about it. I should have blanked my expression before getting into the car. I didn't want to raise any unnecessary fears for him or anyone, so I lied.

"It's nothing. I'm just a little nervous now that we're heading to New York."

"I understand," James said as he placed his hand on mine. His hands dwarfed mine considerably, but for the first time, I noticed the similarities between his fingers and mine. I turned my face to look at him and nodded in affirmation, his eyes were a little downcast but were filled with understanding. He was a good person in a bad situation.

"New York, here we come," James said as he turned the key in the ignition before backing out of the driveway.

Chapter 9
The Road Trip

"It's almost a two-hour drive to New York, we'll be there around noon," I said as soon as we were on the highway again. It seemed like a lifetime ago, we were hauling from Florida to North Carolina, then to New Jersey. Our road trip would soon be coming to an end in a few hours, and we still did not look like we were prepared to take on Mandala. Hell, we had no idea what we were up against yet.

I glanced into the side mirror to check the others. I could only see Amy and Zeke's shoulders. The duo had been quiet for most of the journey, and Zeke had been helping to remind Amy whenever she needed to take her medications. He had already taken an important role in managing the team.

"Hey guys, what are you thinking?" I said as I made eye contact with Amy through the mirror.

"I'm thinking of getting a big fat steak as soon as we are done bringing down Mandala." Zeke volunteered with closed eyes. He was trying to fall asleep.

We all laughed at his remark, it was nice he felt optimistic about the whole thing, a feeling I was not sure I had.

"What about you, Amy?"

"I'm thinking of pumping shots into the asshole who is responsible for my sickness," Amy said with a grin.

"That's the spirit," James said as he blared the Firebird's horn in agreement. We all laughed envisioning Amy's small figure holding her shotgun again.

"What about you, Alice?" Amy asked in her small voice.

"Me?" I stuttered.

"Yeah."

"Well, I don't know yet, but I'm not taking another road trip for a long time. Probably go somewhere with a lot of sun." I answered with a coy smile.

"And you James? What would you do?"

James turned to stare at me for a while as if his answer was written on my face. I guess he did not want to say anything that would seem like he was abandoning me again.

"I'm not sure myself, but what I know is that I'll pay more attention to the things that matter the most."

I looked in James' direction and nodded indicating to him that I understood. Somehow, the road trip had leeched out whatever anger I felt toward him, and I was thankful for it. I could not wait to end this and go back to the way we were before all the craziness. I knew it wouldn't be the same without my mom, but I had a feeling we would make it work somehow.

After sharing our thoughts and plans, we all soon fell into silence, as the Firebird sped along the highway. By the time I glanced into the side mirror Amy was already asleep, and I could see Zeke resting his head on Amy's shoulder fast asleep. Something about the way they both slept brought a smile to my face. It reminded me of how I always ended up sleeping on Mom while watching TV. It also reminded me that life goes on even in the most dire circumstances.

"Alice." James' voice snapped me out of my reveries.

"Yeah, what's up?" I answered as I turned to look at him.

"You know I'm really sorry about everything. I wish I could have explained everything to you before I left, but I felt I was keeping us all safe by not telling you anything. Felicity understood why I had left, but I guess the knowledge was not enough to keep her from feeling sad. The uncertainty of my survival and the fact that she was unable to reach me must have gotten to her. But that's all behind us now. She's in a better place. I'm sure she'll be looking down at you with pride.

This company, it's evil, and if we had known any better in the beginning, we wouldn't have had anything to do with them. They had promised their experiments were not going to harm you, only help you." He paused for a while to analyze my expression before continuing. My mind was still processing everything he was saying. As much as I tried to understand where he was coming from, the feeling of abandonment had hit me hard. I had grown a dependency for him at that time, and his sudden disappearance took a toll on Mom and me.

I knew he was doing what he thought was best, but I still had to wonder how things would have turned out if we had all dealt with the situation together. It was naïve to think it would have had a different ending for Mom, a better ending, but the thought weighed on me. "I don't want you to think we did it for the money. It was nothing like that. Your mother and I loved you very much. As soon as we got wind that their experiments were beginning to have a toll on you, we wanted out. But Mandala, the head of the operation, came to us explaining how we had to do some more tests to be certain you would be okay. We were prepared to take you away forcefully, but we were concerned about your health, so we waited. By the time we were sure they were doing more harm than good, it was too late."

"I'm not getting something. I thought you didn't come along to stay with us until my dad died. What am I not getting?" I asked more confused than ever.

"Alice, there are some things that you were not aware of for a long time. We kept them from you, thinking you'd be safer and better off not knowing anything."

"Like the fact that I was experimented on?"

"Yeah, we planned to tell you, but when you were much older."

"There you go using the pronoun, what's with this 'we' stuff?" I asked beginning to get irritated. It seemed like he was just going around in circles.

"It might sound very -"

While James was still trying to explain, we were jolted by a truck ramming into the back of the Firebird. Immediately, Zeke and Amy were propelled forward waking them from their slumber. They were just as confused as we were. James gripped the steering wheel with white knuckles in order to keep the Firebird under control.

"What was that?" Amy asked in a startled voice.

I glanced in the mirror, but I could only make out the vehicle that had rammed us from behind. It was an ash colored pick-up truck.

"Alice, I think it's your friend again, and this time she has a partner," James said as he peered into the rearview mirror.

"What the hell is her problem?" I shouted out angrily. James and I stared at each other in shock. These people who worked for Mandala were persistent.

"Who are you talking about?" Amy asked looking puzzled. Zeke had to explain to Amy about our earlier encounter with her.

"Seems she likes to play rough," Amy said as she glanced back to take a look at the truck. The truck was now gaining speed and slipstreaming the Firebird. "Felicity" was behind the wheel, and an angry looking man was leaning out of the passenger window. Felicity directed the truck to the right side of the Firebird and was now straddling two lanes. The truck got closer and without warning bumped into the side of the Firebird.

The angry looking man mouthed some words in our direction which were unfathomable in the heat of the moment. But it was clear, they meant business and were trying to stop us. In that instance, I recognized who the man was. He was the man from the funeral who had taken my ring. We had been followed all along. It didn't just begin with Felicity.

"What are we going to do now?" Zeke asked as he leaned forward in his seat.

"Everyone put your seatbelts on. I'll try to outrun them, but it might get really bumpy." James said as he put the Firebird into a lower gear, which made the engine roar harder than I have ever thought possible. As James tasked the engine of the Firebird, we started gaining distance on the truck. Our plan was now obvious to the duo in the truck as they attempted to keep up with the Firebird, but it was proving to be a difficult task. I remembered my mom had told me how my dad had tuned the engine of the Firebird to the extent it could outrace NASCAR vehicles. I always thought that it was just something she toyed about with me as a kid, but I now understood the reality of it.

As the truck fell into our rearview once again, we all cheered for James. It was a sort of mini victory. Just when we thought we had won a battle, the truck came into view again. From my mirror, I could see Felicity's passenger climb out of the moving truck through the window and make his way to the open bed of the vehicle.

"What's he doing?" I asked no one in particular as I stared into the mirror.

"I have no idea," James answered.

"It looks like he's pushing something out from the back of the truck." Amy offered an explanation for the man's actions.

Apparently, Amy was correct. From my mirror, I saw some heavy metal roll onto the highway from the back of the truck. They looked like heavy-duty axles. As soon as he was done dumping them onto the highway. The man climbed back into the passenger seat through the window.

"They are crazier than they look," Amy said in a surprised voice.

It was now obvious the man had let the metal off the truck to lighten their vehicle's load. They were now gaining on the Firebird despite its incredible speed.

The truck was now about 200 yards away from us when we heard a loud crack go off.

"Was that a gun?"

Before Zeke's question could be answered by anyone, we heard the sound again, canceling any doubts, whatsoever.

"Holy shit." I turned back in my seat focusing on the road ahead. James was engrossed with putting as much distance between us and the truck as possible. He did not glance in my direction.

"That's definitely a gun," Amy said as she grabbed her duffel bag from the car floor.

Another shot rang out, and it hit the passenger side mirror, shattering it to smithereens. I ducked down in fear. The mirror was so close that I could have easily been shot.

I was thinking of calling Finn to help us out as he had before, but we could not afford to slow down to take a look at the license plate of the truck. I was still going through other possible options in my mind when I saw Amy pull out the shotgun from her duffel bag. I had never been happier to see a gun in my life. She got out the shells from her bag and began loading them into the gun. While she was still loading the gun, another shot rang out. This time it was followed by a loud blast. The Firebird immediately slumped to the left side.

"Damn! They've nicked a tire." James said in anger as he fisted the steering wheel.

"What are we going to do now?" I asked with a slight look of dejection, knowing there was no way we could outrun them now.

"I've got an idea," Amy said before pausing for us to listen in on her plan. She rolled down her window till it could not go down any further then adjusted herself on the seat.

"James, I need you to slow down enough to get me level with the truck. I'm going to shoot out all of their tires." She finished off, cocking the shotgun simultaneously.

Although Amy looked innocent without an ounce of intimidation in her, her ocean eyes were now filled with so much intensity, there was almost no sign of the former Amy in them.

"Are you sure about this?" James asked her, as he stared at her through the rearview mirror.

"Hundred percent. This is our only chance." She replied.

"OK. Are you ready?"

"Yeah."

My heart was beginning to race, knowing that getting to New York alive was tethered to this moment. James slowly eased up on the gas, and the truck closed in on us slowly.

300 yards, 250, 200, 150.

"Getting closer, almost there," Amy said with one hand on the shotgun. The shotgun was lying on her lap. She was going to take them on by surprise, since they had no knowledge we had a weapon with us.

100 yards. 50 yards.

The man with the gun was now side to side with Amy's window. He was grinning at her, totally oblivious to what was about to happen. In one quick fluid motion, Amy got the gun up from her lap and raised it to the window. The grin on his face was immediately replaced with a confused look. It was obvious he did not see it coming. Amy squeezed the trigger, and a deafening noise erupted in the vehicle. The recoil from the gun jerked Amy backward violently.

But she had been prepared for it, she regained her position and squeezed the trigger again. The truck swerved sharply to the right and ran off of the road before Amy could get off the third shot. The truck was now falling behind the Firebird once again.

"Yeah! Yeah!" We all shouted in pure excitement. Two tires shot was better than nothing.

"How do you like that?" Amy shouted out of the window.

"We have to get to a gas station and change our tire before they do." I quickly pulled out my phone to map the nearest gas station.

"Where did you learn to shoot like that Amy?" James asked with his face lit up in smiles.

"From my dad. We used to go hunting together."

I glance into the only side mirror to confirm Felicity was no longer on our tail.

"I don't think Felicity will be bothering us again. At least for now."

"Yeah, you're right. But now they'll be expecting us. I hope Finn's approach works out." James said looking in my direction.

"There's going to be a gas station in a mile on the right. Do you think the car can make it?" I winced as I thought about all of the damage the Firebird had just endured.

"It should. We'll change the tire there and keep going."

James turned off the road, and we were now heading in the direction of the gas station. The gas station turned out to be a small family owned station. We were the only customers in sight. The owner was a middle-aged man and changed the tires without asking any questions. We were all grateful for that. The spare tire in the trunk of the Firebird was already flat, so the man pumped it before fixing it. After inspecting the shot tire, he told us we were going to need a new tire and rim since the rim had sustained so much damage. James paid him, and we all thanked him before getting back into the car. It was already past noon by the time we got back to the highway. The unforeseen incident had cost us, and we were already falling behind the schedule. James pushed the engine of the Firebird to its limits as we hurried toward New York. After about thirty minutes of driving, we could make out the signature landscape view of the city.

Skyscrapers in the distance were now visible, which indicated we were getting closer to our destination. As soon as we were within the city limits, I called Finn to let him know we would soon be arriving at our destination. Our plan of getting in and staying unnoticed was all hinged on Finn. He picked up on the first ring and informed me he was on standby and waiting to get into action.

"Is he ready?" James asked as he turned the highway to connect to the city.

"Yeah, Finn's always ready," I replied.

"This is it guys, we are headed to the camp."

PART TWO

Chapter 10
The Kidnapping

Hours before the youth homeless shelter's alarm blared, Maya and Caleb collected their change to see how much money they had made in the past week from odd jobs and begging on various street corners. The pair had no money to their names and were limited in how they could acquire money and sustenance.

They lived from one meal to the next. Aged 16, both of them were typical teenagers that you would find living in youth shelters and working the streets in Maryland. Minutes before the alarm bellowed, Derek, the bully of the shelter, approached Maya and Caleb as they counted their money with the intent to rob them.

Although money was scarce, any cent counted. This behavior was typical of Derek. He waited till the sun set when everyone had done their fair share of begging on the streets. Finding an easy way to get money, he would roam the shelter for spare change or bully any vulnerable teens he could rob.

Seconds before the alarm made all the teens deaf, Caleb landed a punch across Derek's face, an act that he had wanted to do since he arrived at the shelter. It had been a long time coming, and Caleb's temper couldn't hold out anymore. After only being at this shelter for a couple of weeks, he had grown an intense hatred toward Derek. When the alarm sounded, the teenagers stopped in their tracks. Confusion led to panic, and soon, everyone was running around to different corners.

Maya, Caleb, and Derek were all frozen in their positions and were all wondering the same thing. Was the alarm because of their altercation? When guards clothed in white padded bodysuits entered the building in an organized formation, it became clear that their worlds were about to be turned upside down. Although Derek was furious and holding his bloodied nose, his fear got the best of him, and he ran back for his cot to retrieve and secure his belongings.

The youth homeless shelter housed a little over 50 kids at a time. Paint was chipping off the walls, and you were considered lucky if you only saw two rats in one day. The setup seemed chaotic to any outsider. Anywhere you stepped was probably invading someone's privacy. Only a few of the luckier ones had actual cots to sleep on. The rest of the children were on air mattresses and sleeping bags sharing the limited amount of blankets available every night. It wasn't one of the nicer ones Maya and Caleb had stayed at, but they had no choice. They go where they find work and stay where they can. In the chaos, Caleb grabbed Maya's hand, and they immediately took off for the back entrance of the building.

Caleb could feel the clamminess of Maya's hand as she shivered from a combination of fear and shock. He dragged her along as adrenaline consumed his body, pushing himself into a full sprint. The shelter had turned into pure chaos. Maya turned her head back only to see guards forcefully constraining the other teens of the shelter and leading them out of the building.

Maya and Caleb couldn't have known what was going on. They only knew that it would put them in danger if they were captured. Everyone was rushing around in a frenzy. Some people were shoving their few belongings in their pockets and bags with the false hope that they would be able to keep their sentimental items somehow. Maya and

Caleb had made a deal early on into their friendship. Knowing that their lives revolved around moving, they decided to now consider only inanimate objects as forms of sentiment. They couldn't continue to drag an abundance of belongings along with them everywhere. They went simple because it reminded them of a better time. They had to be smarter than that and just rely on their memories. Cots and sleeping bags were being turned upside down by the teens in an attempt to block off the guards. The guards held batons and were not sympathetic to even the youngest of the children, beating them with no remorse. They came here for a reason, and they were determined to carry it out perfectly.

Some cries and shouts were blended and forgotten in between the echoes of the alarm that still bounced off of the walls of the shelter. The alarm was so loud that Maya wondered if the whole world could hear it. They finally reached the back door, and to no surprise, it wasn't only their idea. Many teens had now gathered toward that door in an attempt to flee, but it was locked shut.

Maya's breathing quickened. She could feel herself hyperventilating, blocking her from coming up with any idea of their escape. "What do we do, where do we go?" Her heart raced, and she noticed dribbles of sweat sliding down Caleb's face, too.

None other than Derek was at the door. He was one of the many that attempted to shove all of his belongings into his pockets. Maya and Caleb's brown money bag hung from his overstuffed pant pocket. "Everyone push!" He shouted loud enough for the rest of them to hear over the blast of the alarm.

The teens obeyed, and in a synchronized fashion, they all shoved the door. After several attempts of doing this, the door finally gave way and flung open, revealing a sea of guards in white. There was no way to turn back now. The teens rushed the guards and attempted to scatter away, hoping to find a gap for their escape. The winter whipped at their skin as the wind rushed inside toward them. This year had brought a brutal cold front.

Caleb and Maya, leaving in such a hurry, definitely did not leave while appropriately clothed for the outside. Their cheeks and noses received an instant brush of pink. There was no time for second thoughts, though. Their turn for exiting the building was approaching, and the guards from inside the shelter were on their heels. As soon as their boots hit the outside ground, they took off toward the left, hoping to reach the wooded area that surrounded the backside of the shelter. However, again, they were not the only ones with such an idea. Many of the children began running toward the trees for cover, but the guards were tailing them. The sea of guards blended with the thick layer of snow that covered the ground, making it even more difficult to spot them.

Everyone appeared to be running in slow motion as their boots trudged through the snow. Even if the teens managed to escape right now, there was no way anyone would survive the night out in the cold. Caleb and Maya still held hands as they kicked through the snow. As they began to approach the beginning of the forest, they quickly looked around for any opportunities to go unnoticed.

Heading toward the west side that appeared to be the least littered by guards, they spotted Derek's large build as he trudged between the leafless trees. His pockets jingled with their coins, making himself a target.

"Idiot," Maya thought to herself. Greed will get him killed.

It almost seemed as if Derek would be able to escape until he came across a large oak tree, and a guard stepped out from behind it tripping him.

Maya and Caleb winced as Derek fell with a large thud, seemingly disappearing into the snow. The guard pulled out his baton, whacking Derek's back for assurance. He grabbed his arms and lifted him with surprising ease as he walked him toward a semi-truck that had been waiting at the back of the building.

Caleb and Maya turned to see the guards quickly piling the teens into the truck. The commotion was distracting them from escaping. The teens were disappearing from the snow, leaving only guards. It looked as if no one had escaped. Caleb and Maya were surrounded now, but they still had to try. They ran into the forest desperately. They knew they would get caught.

They knew that they would end up in the semi with the rest of the kids from the shelter, but they couldn't give up now. The pair held onto the sliver of hope that they would be the only ones to make it out. They ran as fast as their legs could carry them through the snow. Their hands became glued to each other from the cold. It was impossible to let go. Maya could barely hear the guard that was quickly approaching behind them because of the heaviness of her breathing. However, Caleb heard it loud and clear, and he was preparing to sacrifice himself for Maya to escape. Caleb slowed his pace, placing himself behind Maya so that she was leading. The guard reached him, and instead of sticking out an arm to grab Caleb, he struck Caleb's back with a baton.

"Run Maya!" He shouted through shivering breaths as he forced himself to release his grip on Maya's hand.

Maya looked back, and shock filled her honey-colored eyes. She was torn between continuing to run and going back for Caleb.

"Run! Maya, please!" Caleb begged now. Maya knew she had to run. Her heart ached with regret, but she knew whatever was going on here, she wouldn't survive. She thrust herself forward into the trees and ran through the tears that stained her face. The cold whipped at her throat, and her eyes were glossy. She was losing vision in the forest. Maya couldn't survive without Caleb by her side. She knew this.

Maya couldn't hear anything anymore besides the sounds of her breathing. She couldn't hear Caleb, couldn't hear the roar of the semi, nor the sounds of the guards.

She could see the other end of the forest now. "I'm going to make it, I'm going to make it." She chanted this into her head, determined to escape this disaster. She wiped the tears that blurred her vision and pushed on. She wanted so badly to collapse and give up. Her body dragged now. She was in no shape to be sprinting for her life at the peak of winter. Her aching legs carried her forward with the determination to call for help once she escaped.

Her thoughts distracted herself from reality and from her surroundings. Her lack of observance may have cost her life. Two batons struck her body at such a force that she collapsed and sunk into the snow with ease. Maya was dazed and confused. Her wet eyes opened and were blinded by an overwhelming sea of white. The only thing recognizable was the bright stain of crimson seeping into the snow. "Is that my blood?" She couldn't tell if she had spoken it or thought this to herself as darkness consumed her.

When Maya woke up, she was inside the semi-truck that was utterly dark. Caleb was at her side, stabilizing her from the vehicle's intense sway. She forced herself to sit up and take in her surroundings.

"How long has it been?" She asked Caleb while wiping the sleep from her eyes. "About two hours. We have no idea where we're going or how long it'll take. The guards aren't telling us anything." Caleb had the look of defeat across his face. He wanted so badly for at least Maya to escape, and now they were both trapped in this truck, deprived of fresh air with who knows how many other people.

Everyone sat on the ground, hugging their knees and trying to avoid toppling over one another on sharp turns. The air was sticky, and there was absolutely no room to wiggle. Thankfully, Caleb and Maya were some of the few lucky ones that were perched against the wall of the truck. At the least, they could relax their backs. Maya's back was still incredibly stiff and bruised from taking the whacks from the batons.

She winced in pain as she tried to readjust herself into a more comfortable position for the unknown duration of the journey ahead of them. Maya was frustrated and angry. "How does no one know what the hell is going on?" Her mind raced at every possibility. But nothing prepared her for what was actually to come.

A familiar face suddenly met hers.

Derek.

But unlike all the other times they had confronted each other, Derek's face showed signs of panic. Maya felt Caleb tense next to her, already balling his hands into fists as if earlier wasn't enough. Derek was known around the shelter to be a bully, and Caleb was one of the rare breeds who would actually fight back.

"What, Derek?" Maya hissed. No one had been talking out of fear of the guards. As soon as Maya's voice was heard, everyone's attention turned to her. The only other sound that could be heard was from the rumble of the truck. "Now is not the time," she warned.

"Listen," he whispered to try to lessen the number of eyes that were on them now.

"They have to stop for gas or the bathroom at some point, right? We have to figure out how to escape then."

For a meathead, he did have a point. It didn't seem like anyone was willing to go down easily. The message was slowly passed along using whispers, doing their best not to draw any attention from the guards.

Suddenly a timid voice was heard from a younger girl in the middle of the sea of kids. "When will we be stopping for the restrooms?" Everyone turned themselves to face the guards. It was a good question, and now that she mentioned it, they all suddenly had the urge to go and relieve themselves.

"We will not be stopping." One of the guards firmly stated. This caused a panic that turned into an uprising in the truck. Everyone began shouting, and some even attempted to stand up.

"We need to be let out now." Derek threatened. His deep voice bellowed. As badly as Caleb and Maya wanted out, Maya couldn't stand to get struck again. They watched the uprising play out in front of them, as they considered better plans.

Suddenly Maya had it. She tugged on Derek's shirt, forcing him to kneel down beside her. "Make them all rush the back door." It was the same plan they had when they were still inside the shelter, but maybe this time, it would have a better outcome. It was plenty more dangerous, but the conditions called for more desperate measures now.

Above the shouting, Derek rose again. And this time, he yelled with such a roar that even Maya got scared. Caleb held onto her tight, knowing that if this plan worked, they could easily be trampled on or shoved out of the truck while moving. They had no way of knowing if they were on a highway or back roads. At once, everyone began lurching forward. The truck trembled under the weight.

"Together!" Derek shouted. The guards pulled out their batons and began making their way to the front by striking people out of their way.

"Again!"

The crowd relentlessly shoved forward, throwing their bodies into each other and at the door. A hinge snapped from the bottom right of the door, causing everyone to cheer.

"Again!"

Another bolt became loose. The guards were striking people even harder now, but the survival instinct and the will to live kept the teenagers motivated.

"Again!"

And just like that, the door bent in and flew off of the truck. Everyone was shoving with such a force, that the impact of the door flying off caused a domino effect. People began falling out of the still moving truck, trampling each other. Caleb still held his grip on Maya, and just as Derek was about to fall out behind the others, Maya found the strength to grab him.

The truck finally came to a sudden halt. This was their opportunity. They ran to the end of the truck, avoiding the guards, and jumped off together. Those who had fallen from the truck were slowly gathering themselves again and attempting to flee in all directions. Once Maya, Caleb, and Derek made it outside, they realized that they had been a little too late. The truck had already made it to its destination.

They looked out to their surroundings. They were in the center of a field surrounded by electric fences topped with barbed wire. And beyond that, trees. Ahead of them were two buildings that were connected by a walkway, and many guards surrounded them. This was a defeat. They were trapped. Out beyond, an unfamiliar silver-haired man was marching toward the frantic teenagers. He placed his hands up in a motion to the guards, to halt their aggressiveness. The semi-truck took off, leaving just the teenagers, guards, and the mysterious man in the camp. Fresh snowfall had begun adding another layer to the already thick platform beneath them. Caleb and Maya stood at each other's sides in anticipation, never unlatching their hands. They still had absolutely no clue what was going on or where they were. Derek stood with arms crossed as if his attitude would be enough to do something.

Everyone else had mixed facial expressions of fright and hopelessness, as the man finally reached them. Heads were turning sporadically as if a sudden exit would appear out of nowhere. A few people even tried to chase after the semi and hop on it, as if it would take them to a better destination. These people had no such luck. Guards were quickly at their sides, pulling them off, nails clawing at the metal of the truck in desperation, in fear, and in agony.

Once the screams and cries of those who refused to give up were finally silenced, the teenagers were met by the silver-haired man. Maya immediately felt chills go through her body as if she was being warned.

Danger. Danger. Danger.

"Hello, everyone." He greeted everyone with a warm smile, but his steel-gray eyes told otherwise.

There was a long pause before he continued. Everyone was stunned, taking in the sound of his voice, his towering height, and silver-flecked hair. He peered around at them slowly, allowing everyone to study his slivers of cold, hateful eyes.

Finally, he spoke.

"My name is Dr. Mandala. I'm sure you're all wondering why you're here. There is nothing to be afraid of. We are here to give you a place to live and learn." His speech gave hope to the younger bunch but brought doubt to those who were older and wearier. They had explicitly chosen kids from a homeless shelter. He knew that almost anything would seem better to them.

"Learn what?" Derek spat, arms still crossed. He was part of the older bunch. And definitely the weariest. Although he was known around the shelter as the bully, he seemed to take on a more protective role suddenly. Was it fear for his own safety, or fear for everyone's safety? Maya wondered. A guard made a move toward Derek, but Mandala stopped him with another motion of his hand. Maya assumed it was an attempt to show Derek that he was concerned for his safety, but she knew better.

"We have recruited you all to give you a new worth, and to make you a better fit for this society we live in today." Everything that came out of the silver-haired man's mouth was vague. No one was getting any real answers. All they understood now was that they had been kidnapped for reasons yet to be discovered.

Recruited?

Society?

What was happening within the society that children and teenagers were to help with?

It was evident that the North was struggling with the recent recession. There were uncountable mass shootings, leading to acts of violence and outrage in major cities such as Chicago, New York City, and Boston. Everyone felt clueless. Everyone in the shelters would just sit and wait around all day until someone finally came by with the news that was passed on from person to person about the current status of the country. Were these rumors ever confirmed? No. Never. Everyone just had to live with a false sense of comfort that at least some news was spread around that day. For the past year, there was no clarity. But had things really gotten so bad that kids were being "recruited"? What could a bunch of kids from a homeless shelter possibly be capable of?

Maya and Caleb felt uneasy. Not only was the entire situation illegal and unethical, but this man was also creating an illusion to persuade a bunch of kids to follow his orders blindly. She wondered if anything that was happening could even be stopped. Would anyone be looking for them? These were kids from a shelter. They could easily be brushed under the rug if need be.

"If you'll all follow me, we will get you cleaned up and placed into your rooms." He turned on his heels and marched back toward the west building he emerged from, while the guards "encouraged" everyone to follow. Some stragglers in the back still searching for any potential escape routes received blows to their backs by batons. Their grunts and cries echoed, but Mandala pretended not to hear them.

Chapter 11
Mandala

Maya gazed up at the tall glass buildings that seemed to stretch for miles into the sky. Looking up at them made her dizzy. The clouds mainly hid the sun, but what little light shone through reflected off of the mirrored buildings. They were almost too hard to look at. Their shape seemed to be octagonal, and Maya couldn't help but admire the architecture. A silver "M" logo stood at the top of both buildings.

"M for Mandala?" She thought to herself.

She and Caleb exchanged no words as they were herded into the building. The only thing they were thankful for was getting out of the frigid winter air and the fact that they were still together. With each of their breaths, a cloud of smoke pooled in front of their faces. Everyone shivered from the lack of proper clothing for the winter. The conditions looked as if they had gone further north.

They finally reached the doors, and Mandala placed a key card onto an electronic pad outside of the glass double doors. The electronic pad clicked green signaling clearance, and he stood back slightly to give the doors room to swing open. As everyone entered the shiny building, a sudden puff of air conditioning sucked them inside.

There was no warm welcome as boys and girls were immediately split off into two lines - guys on the left and girls on the right. Maya reached for Caleb in confusion and fear, but a guard quickly ripped them apart as if he had known they'd have trouble separating. They kept their eyes glued on each other as they were herded into different rooms. Maya followed the rest of the girls into a room that had showers, medical examiners, medical beds, medical equipment, and stacks of gray uniforms.

Everything in the room had the same shine and metallic appearance that outsides of the buildings had. Maya wondered how new these facilities were. It was as if someone had just taken off the plastic wrapping. Her eyes moved around frantically, trying to take in all of her surroundings. How many staff were in this room? Why were there medical examiners? Her mind was moving at a rapid pace leading to more confusion. Nothing was being explained, and it was making her feel insane. She wasn't one to give in to things without questioning. Her entire existence was plagued with the word "why." Not being able to ask made her skin crawl.

Her thoughts were cut brief as a staff member in thick black-rimmed glasses began removing Maya's clothing. Maya's immediate instinct was to slap her hands away.

"Why?" It was all she could manage to come out of her mouth.

The staff member seemed shocked at Maya's reaction. Had other people been more willing?

"Listen, ladies. Let's make this as efficient as possible. Remove your clothing, step into the showers, then come out to a medical examiner. Let's move!" A woman who was pacing with a clipboard began shouting orders. She stood at the center of the room and had curly short blonde hair. She was tall, and her heels clicked through the room against the white tiled floor wherever she walked. Maya assumed she was a doctor based on her white coat that hung low to her thighs.

The staff member motioned again at Maya, but Maya removed her clothing herself, not wanting this stranger to touch her. She used her hands to cover herself as she quickly made her way to the showers. The line was long, and she was getting cold again, but a shower was much needed.

Maya was average height among her peers. She had wide hips, but everything else about her was thin from a lack of proper eating. Her brunette hair fell an inch past her shoulders, and she had thick brown eyebrows that sat above her honey-colored eyes. Her natural olive complexion had grown pale from the winter and was now doused in hues of pinks and reds from the cold.

Goosebumps rose on her skin as she impatiently waited her turn in line. All she could hope for now was a simmering hot shower. That would be the one good thing to come out of this. As she neared her turn in line, she noticed steam coming from the showers, and a smile almost reached her face.

Almost.

She was shoved into the showers by a much taller girl behind her who was obviously tired of waiting. The shove caused Maya to slip and bang her knee against a shower knob. A gash formed in her skin, releasing a gush of blood. No one seemed to see the events unfolding, and if they did, they just didn't care. Maya decided against making a huge scene even though the gash seemed deep, and she was filled with extreme rage at the girl behind her.

Were people already beginning to assert their dominance here? Wasn't everyone united and panicking together not five minutes ago? Everyone had apparently kicked into survival mode, and it was eat or be eaten.

She needed to toughen up.

The stream of water from the shower hid her silent tears as the gash burned from the pressure of the water jets. She quickly shampooed and scrubbed for fear that she would run out of time. Once she completed her shower, she was dried by a staff member and hurried to a medical examiner. She helped herself up onto the table that was covered with a white paper sheet. Her knee still oozed blood, and that was the first thing the examiner noticed. It immediately began dripping onto the sheet in droplets of dark maroon.

The stern woman shook her head in annoyance and cleaned the wound roughly with a washcloth before declaring that it needed stitches.

"No, it doesn't. I'll be fine." Maya spoke up with a shaky voice. She didn't want to get stitches. She didn't know how severe the pain would be, and she wasn't ready to reveal any weakness to the surrounding girls.

Before Maya even had a chance to get off of the table, the medical examiner was already poking her with a needle and thread. It did hurt just as she'd expected, but now was an opportunity to show her strength. She held in any pain she felt and balled her hands into fists. To prevent herself from screaming, she chewed on her tongue. Needles made her nauseous, and the last thing she wanted to do was watch this stranger sew her up, so she stared up at the ceiling and counted the tile squares.

Thirty-eight she counted.

"All done. It just needed five stitches," the medical examiner replaced her gloves and moved onto other parts of Maya's body to inspect.

"It just needed five stitches." Maya mocked in her head.

"You'll need to see me again in one week so that I can remove them." Her annoyance was as if she'd heard Maya. She analyzed Maya's body front and back for anything else suspicious and took her time to press her fingers into Maya's bruises on her back.

"The guards, huh." The lady mumbled to herself. She seemed familiar with these bruises as if they were a common sight. That made Maya uneasy. She decided not to respond since she was not here to please the staff.

"And what are these from?"

Maya shivered as her fingers brushed over the scars on the sides of her stomach. She knew that the medical examiner already knew what they were. They were obvious. The scars were in perfect circles of cigarette butts. The clump of them on her right side almost made a flower.

Maya gave her no answer.

She couldn't explain to a random stranger how her mother had abused her as a child, how Maya had to raise herself from such a young age to take care of herself and her mother's drug addiction. She couldn't tell this random stranger that she had been used as her mother's ashtray.

She needed to stay inconspicuous and unremarkable in this place. She didn't want to be seen as a target for rebellion, or have any eyes on her. It was bad enough she was beginning to be associated with Caleb. Chances were they would be separated in one way or another. The thought caused panic and despair in Maya.

After the medical examiner was done violating her body and had dismissed her hesitantly, Maya changed into a gray, bland uniform that consisted of light gray pants and a matching light gray polo. All that was left to wonder now was if Caleb was going through the same thing. She hoped none of the guys had also decided to prove their dominance, but she knew better.

She was pulled out of her thoughts as a bright flash went off in her face. A camera?

Maya was left stunned.

"Come sign here." A pen and clipboard were shoved into her hands. The next line on the page consisted of a six-digit number where she assumed she should sign.

Mayhem Greene.

Once all of the girls and guys had completed their very personal examinations and dressed in their uniforms, they were led by guards across the walkway into the east building. The lines finally meshed, and Maya and Caleb easily found their way to each other. It was as if they were magnets with opposite polar ends. Maya quickly scanned over Caleb to assess for any injuries and saw blue bruises forming on his knuckles. This didn't surprise her.

Better someone else than him, Maya thought. She'd ask him about it later. The snow was falling faster now, and all Maya could think about was her mom's voice yelling at her as a toddler not to go out in the cold with wet hair or she'd get sick. "If only you could see me now," she wondered.

But Maya knew that wasn't a possibility. Her mom had abandoned her at a young age after getting involved with too many drugs. She only ever cared about Maya's well-being if it meant that it could potentially cost her unnecessary money, like getting sick from having wet hair in the cold. Her hands folded into fists at the memory of her mom. When everyone finally piled into the first-floor hallway, key cards were being passed around for everyone.

Names were being called.

"Caleb Darius."

Caleb raised his hand and was given his card. His picture, room number, and six-digit identification number were printed neatly on it.

A few more names were called, and Maya waited impatiently.

"Mayhem Greene."

Maya stepped up to get her badge.

Derek immediately swung around cackling. He was already back to his old ways.

"Mayhem?" he snarled.

She had instant regret for writing her full name on the paper, but it was her instinct that took over. Her drugged-out mother obviously named her mayhem, and it pretty much served as an oxymoron thus far in her life. She never caused any mayhem, as many that met her had expected. To avoid continuing to let down others, she decided to stick with Maya.

He'll get over it, she hoped. But in reality, she knew she would never live this down for the duration of their stay there. Caleb squeezed her shoulders to calm her, which worked. The next name she was called. "Miles Ray."

When Maya caught sight of his face, it was obvious that a black eye was forming. He was equal with Caleb in height and build, but the weaker opponent.

A fair fight, she thought to herself.

She felt Caleb's hands tense around her shoulders.

"Was it before or after the picture was taken?" she whispered to him.

"Before." he smiled at the fact that she already knew what had happened.

For the first time in a while and in the most unexpected place, Maya laughed.

Chapter 12
The Welcome

"Alright, everyone." Some other superior was speaking to everyone now. It was the doctor from Maya's examination room.

"These are access cards to your rooms. You will be sharing them with three other people. My advice is to get along because there will be no switching rooms. There will be no tolerance of guys in the girl's rooms and vice versa after 9 pm every night. Go get acquainted."

And with that, everyone was hustling and bustling throughout the hallway, trying to locate their rooms and roommates.

"Please, for god sake, do not put me in Derek's room." Caleb had his fingers crossed, and he was continuing to make Maya laugh. Her laugh from earlier was like sunshine to his ears, and he wanted to keep hearing it.

"What's your room number?" she turned to him, reaching out for his badge.

"110, and you?" he asked as they walked down the hallway together.

"103."

Their silence confirmed that they were annoyed that their rooms weren't closer together but also felt unanimous satisfaction that they weren't further apart.

"Oh no." Maya squeezed Caleb's arm as she noticed Miles scan into room 110.

"Of course." He groaned.

They parted ways, and Maya left him with a warning to take it easy. They didn't need any more enemies than they already had on day one.

Maya scanned into 103 and took a deep breath before entering.

She was the last of the bunch to enter. Three sets of fearful eyes met her.

"Mayhem?" the redhead asked, clearly remembering Derek's outburst from the hall.

"Please call me Maya." She stuck out her hand to meet everyone.

"I'm Faye," the redhead's curls bounced as she shook Maya's hand. Her skin was pale and clothed in red freckles. She was taller than Maya by two inches and more filled out.

"I'm Danielle, and this is Eva." Clear glasses framed Danielle's smooth dark complexion. She had an athletic build and seemed to tower over her friend Eva. Eva was much shorter than the other girls and had naturally curly, brunette hair and full bangs that curtained her face. Her gray uniform hung off of her petite body.

"Okay, so Faye, Danielle, and Eva. Easy enough." Maya cracked a smile, trying to warm up to everyone. Repeating things helped to jog her memory into action.

"I'll take the top bunk if you don't mind," Faye said while already halfway up the metal ladder, eager to claim her space.

"Go for it." Maya preferred the bottom anyway. She tended to move in her sleep and would have probably fallen off of the top bunk at some point or another.

Danielle and Eva unarguably picked their beds on the other side of the room.

Together, the four girls opened the closets, drawers, and mini-fridge, which all appeared to be bare despite the four bundles of hygiene products set aside neatly for the girls on each bed.

No one came with any other belongings, it seemed.

"Everyone to the hallway," an announcement blared through the intercoms throughout the first floor of the east building.

The girls obeyed, and everyone quietly filed out into the hall, unsure of what would happen next. The hall was crowded now, and Maya turned to see Caleb stuck between too many people to be able to reach her. They gave each other reassuring nods that they were okay.

"We will now be giving a tour of the upstairs where your classes will be held, as well as all of your meals. After the tour, we will have dinner, discuss your schedules, and then be released for curfew." The woman that had attempted to unclothe Maya in the medical examiner room spoke with authority. She seemed too timid to be leading such a large group, but Maya figured they gave this job to less important personnel.

Was this some sort of boarding school? What did she mean by classes? Maya's brows furrowed in confusion and annoyance. She guessed that this was what Mandala meant by learning.

Together, everyone climbed the stairs to the second floor, and Caleb finally found a way to squirm past the endless sea of puzzled faces to reach Maya. They walked together in silence as the group entered the second floor and halted. The woman pushed open two double doors on her right, revealing a large dining hall that seemed too fancy for a bunch of kids.

The dining hall followed the modern theme of the building and looked too white to eat in, to potentially be covered in smears of bright red and yellow condiments. There were long white tables surrounded by silver stools that were nailed to the floor. Everything looked pristine.

"Are we the first to eat here?" Maya wondered contemplating the possibility of them being the first to endure this specific *"boarding school."*

"Breakfast, lunch, and dinner will be served here at 8 am, 1 pm, and 5 pm. Each meal will be for an hour. If you are late, you will not be given a meal."

There was no room for any questions, by the way she spoke. Every word was harsh even from her timid self as if the children stepping out of line would lead to consequences for her. Everything seemed like orders. Nothing here was an offer.

The group shuffled through the hallway.

"There's a door that says 'Staff Only' to your left. Do not ever try to go into them."

Maya and Caleb scanned the rooms carefully, but the windows were blacked out. Being told not to go into them sparked their curiosity.

"And in the second half of the hallway are your classrooms."

The group walked more until they reached the further wing.

"This is where you will learn mathematics, science, and economics." She pointed to the same classroom.

"And here is where you will spend the majority of your time, learning about the capabilities of humanity."

How much more vague can these people possibly be? Maya thought. Everything was a blur in her mind.

Capabilities of humanity?

"We will now head back to the dining hall for dinner. Every weekday, you will have classes from 9:15 am until the end of your humanities class, with meals as your breaks. As stated before, the curfew is at 9 pm."

"What is this? Why are we in school?" Derek dared to speak up.

The timid woman sighed. It was obvious she'd been prepped for this question. "This is a great opportunity for you all. We are giving you better lives than being in a shelter with no money and food." She sounded like a robot. How many times had she practiced that line? Maybe she borrowed Mandala's notes.

"But why?" Someone else from the crowd's voice was heard. It sounded like one of the younger children. Maya's heart ached for the younger group. She knew that they understood nothing, and she wanted to stay strong for them and put on a persona that made everything seem fine. But in reality, it wasn't fine, and Maya had to look at the bigger picture. She needed them all to get out of there. The woman blatantly ignored the child and released everyone to dinner. She looked frustrated and nervous and hurried into one of the 'Staff Only' rooms. It almost seemed as if she were forced to play this role.

Given her permission, everyone filed into the dining hall with grumbling stomachs at the sound of a clock striking 5 pm.

Perfectly timed.

No one had realized how famished they were until they entered the dining hall to a mixture of delicious scents.

Maya and Caleb shuffled to two seats in a corner to try to mask themselves as much as possible while they hashed everything out. Everyone seemed to blend into the silver stools with their bland gray uniforms. The company was making it clear that everyone was seen as equal.

None of the children held a superiority status above others. Despite everyone's different ages, they were viewed as a single entity - all here for Mandala's unknown purpose.

The food was already prepared and placed at each seat in a meticulous manner. The dining hall could fit everyone perfectly as if they'd already been counted beforehand. The food was in silver trays, and everyone received a glass of water. The trays precisely mimicked each other's contents. The food didn't even seem half bad. The pasta tasted decent, the broccoli looked fresh, and the grapes were juicy. Maya hadn't had a meal this refreshing in years. In between large gulps of food and water, Maya and Caleb caught up.

"So, Mandala clearly wants to use us for his benefit... but, we don't know how yet." He began.

"It seems serious if we also have to take classes for whatever plan he has. And I'm also more suspicious because if this place is as good as they all make it out to seem, why couldn't the rich willingly send their kids here, instead of kidnapping a bunch of homeless kids from a shelter?" Maya was digging deep into the situation. Caleb admired her intelligence and detective-like habits.

They couldn't add much on that note since they were still in the dark about the intentions of the facility. They began discussing the people around them. They still didn't know who everyone was from the shelter since the homeless kids filter in and out often, including themselves.

"Okay, so explain why it was necessary to punch Miles." Maya had a smirk on her face. Caleb's natural instinct was always to fight back, so she was curious to see what ticked Caleb off this time. It never really took much.

"It's nothing, he just pissed me off." Caleb was swallowing down his pasta, avoiding making eye contact with Maya. Now Maya was even more curious than ever. She was always told the reasons behind his fights.

"Come on, tell me." She pleaded. She was not going to let this go. Maya scanned the room to find where Miles was seated and saw him at the table next to Derek. His black eye was prominent now, even from their distance.

"I see he and Derek are hitting it off. Maybe they're bonding over both having been punched in the face by you." She commented while turning back to face Caleb. She expected a laugh out of him but received no signs of amusement.

"Come on!" She lightly kicked him under the table, and he rolled his eyes in frustration. Maya was the most stubborn person Caleb knew. This would never end.

"He just made a comment about you. Alright?" Caleb was defeated. She always got her way with him, but she knew this time that was the most she'd get out of him. He couldn't face Maya and explain to her that the reason he punched Miles was that he made a comment that crossed all lines about Maya.

Maya crossed her arms in insecurity. How were they already making enemies? By the anger sprawled onto Caleb's face, she knew it had to be something inappropriate. She was happy that she had Caleb to defend her but also worried that he was fighting her battles for her in too much of a physical way. What if one day, Caleb doesn't win?

She grabbed Caleb's bruised hand and said, "Thank you."

He squeezed her hand in return as reassurance that he didn't need it. The pair finished the rest of their dinner in silence. They hadn't really come to any conclusions about their purpose at Mandala. Their primary concern now was survival amongst all of these people that were beginning to try and claim their dominance. Maya assumed everyone would want to work together to find a way to escape. But, it seemed as if people were slowly adjusting and accepting their fate. Cliques were forming during dinner time, and it was apparent that some of them took the tactic of being goodie-two-shoes with the hope that it would get them far.

"So besides Miles, your roommates are good?" Maya drank the last sip of her water, wanting to change the subject as soon as possible. Everyone was chatting away in the dining hall as dinner was approaching its end.

"Yeah, no one else gave me a problem. How was your situation?"

Maya explained to him that her roommates seemed just as nervous, and she also reluctantly explained what had happened during the medical examination and how she ended up getting five stitches in her knee. Blood immediately rushed to Caleb's face in anger. "Which one is she?" He was scanning the room with his fists on the table.

"Caleb! It's fine, I'm fine, I promise! You can't always do this. I promise you I am okay." Caleb's combative attitude was beginning to worry her. They did not need to become targets this early on.

"Listen, we have to handle ourselves and lay low if we're going to figure out what's going on here and how to escape. No more fights! And I promise I'll be alright." She felt like she was speaking to a child, but this matter was of peak importance, and she couldn't risk Caleb ruining it because he felt the urge to punch someone every time he got mad.

"Let me see it," he looked down at her leg covered in a blur of gray. Maya looked down and noticed a blotch of crimson seeping through at her knee.

"Shit." She rolled up her pants, revealing an apparent infection that was beginning to form. She dabbed a napkin with the rest of Caleb's water and tried to clean the area as much as possible.

"You need to get that cleaned properly. Maya, it looks bad." Caleb's fists were still clenched tight.

"And you should ice that." She commented, finalizing their dispute. If she was expected to take care of herself, he needed to do the same.

Chapter 13
Derek

At exactly 6 pm, the clock sounded, signaling the end of dinner. Everyone filed out of the dining hall haphazardly and headed downstairs to the rooms. Maya hated that she had enjoyed her meal so much. It made it harder to hate the situation they'd been thrown into, but her stomach hadn't felt this satisfied for too long, in fact, for as long as she could remember.

"We have three hours until our curfew." Maya put air quotes around the word curfew. She wasn't sure how seriously they'd take that. 9 pm was so early to stop socializing with each other. The timid woman from before was back in their hallway, making sure everything went smoothly.

"Is this curfew thing serious? We only have a couple of hours left?" As annoying as Derek was, he wasn't afraid to ask the questions that no one else wanted to take credit for. He obviously hadn't gotten Maya's memo about staying unnoticed, but at least he could unknowingly do their dirty work for them. He was bothering the woman that Maya had increasingly grown curious about. She almost felt bad for her.

"Trust me. After humanities, you'll be thankful."

Maya looked up at Caleb with dread taking over her facial features.

Whatever this humanities class was, it was something to fear.

"Let's take a walk." Caleb guided Maya out of the cluster of people, taking his opportunity to scout the place while everyone badgered the poor woman with questions.

"Just talk to me casually, while I count how many cameras there are." Maya understood, and she appreciated that he began taking precautions to protect their identities.

"Alright, well, I noticed that there's only one 'Staff Only' room down here, and I'm starting to think that that woman stays there. She might be here to watch over all of us, but she's also so much quieter than the other staff that I'm starting to consider the possibility that she may be here against her will. Or once was."

Caleb snorted.

"What?" Maya crossed her arms as they continued to make their way down the hallway. She was coming to the realization that this woman could potentially be on their side. It was still way too early to tell, but she needed to keep the possibility in her mind, while she and Caleb continued to develop future plans.

"Nothing, Ms. Detective. I was just wondering how much Criminal Minds you've watched in the past." He laughed and counted four on his fingers. Criminal Minds was always on the TV in the shelters. It became their favorite show.

"I'm the detective? Keep counting your security cameras," Maya was giggling with Caleb now.

She couldn't possibly imagine what life would be like if they ended up separated. Caleb and Maya had been growing up together in foster care homes since they were eleven years old and ran away together after a bad experience at their final home when they turned sixteen. Every decision they had made in the past six years of their life had been for each other. They were each other's weakness and felt like each other's only family left in the world.

"What are you two doing over here?" Derek's annoying voice was suddenly behind them.

"Huh, Mayhem?" He asked again impatiently, clearly trying to get under her skin.

The pair turned around to face him.

"Bite me, Derek." Maya spat at him with a disgusted look on her face. All they've been doing was trying to help Derek, and he continued to disappoint and go back to his inevitable form as the bully of the community.

"Listen. Whatever you guys are planning, I want in on it." His annoying voice now contained hints of desperation. The fact that he was pleading with those who he happened to dislike the most almost brought a grin to Maya's face. Almost.

"We're not planning anything, Derek. Go back to your friends." Caleb placed his hand on Maya's back to lead her forward and away from him. Derek would be the one to sabotage the well-being of others for his own sake. How has he managed to live this long? Maya wondered.

"I'm being serious. If you guys come up with a plan, and I'm not informed, I can promise you that your plan won't go through." Typical Derek, Maya thought. Empty threats following his cries for help.

"I hope the barbed wires cut your ass on the way out."

Maya and Caleb left him to sulk as they headed back to the others.

Chapter 14
The Curfew

Hours went by as they scanned the hallway, observing the timid woman whose name they discovered was Isabella, and cleaning Maya's wound some more in the public bathroom/shower area. The clock struck 9 pm, signaling a supposedly generous curfew.

"Alright, everyone. This curfew doesn't necessarily mean you need to sleep. However, you are required to stay in your rooms." Isabella watched as everyone shuffled into their designated rooms as they familiarized themselves more with their key cards and seemed to be getting the hang of them. Her nerves today had been at an all-time high.

She suddenly felt responsible for nearly eighty children and was plagued with the weight of what would be soon to come for them. She was just getting the hang of the ropes at Mandala and was now being flung full-force into a plan she knew little about. She simply kept reminding herself to watch out for the kids.

Little did Isabella know, Maya had figured her out already. Maya and Caleb said good night and separated into their rooms with a final warning from Maya about not getting physical with Miles again. When Maya and her roommates rejoined, they noticed that the closet was now filled with uniforms fit to their correct sizes, and the dresser contained undergarments, light gray pajama sets, and gray socks.

"What is their obsession with gray?" Faye asked while pulling out her pajama set for the night.

"They want us to look as horrible as possible to diminish our will to live." Maya's joke made Faye, Danielle, and Eva simultaneously combust into laughter. She was happy that they were all getting along well and hoped that they were all able to help keep each other sane.

"Did you guys figure out anything about why we're here?" Maya could tell that these girls seemed genuinely concerned and frightened as she felt. Although, she knew she took a possible risk of trusting them. However, in these circumstances, it was necessary.

"My guess is, this is some type of trade school, and they need us to learn how to create an alternate source of energy or some crap, and we're their only hope." Danielle was climbing up the metal ladder into her top bunk. Danielle must have watched a lot of movies in her time, Maya thought.

Maybe she was right. Maya gave the idea a second to settle in her mind. Perhaps this all isn't as serious as they suspect it to be, and they really are at some sort of boarding school. Maya angled herself cleverly while changing into her cotton gray pajama pants to avoid exposing her knee to her new roommates. She didn't want them to get concerned and potentially rat her out to a staff member. That was not a part of the plan to lay low.

"Yeah, I guess they just wanted to test their new school on a bunch of shelter kids first. It is a safe bet. Who are we gonna tell if it goes to hell?" Maya thought aloud while climbing into her own bed. Even if she and Faye were terribly wrong, it did put her mind slightly at ease. Maybe she would get the much-needed rest they'd all required. She slid under her covers and put pressure on her knee with the uniform shirt she wore earlier. Her knee had been throbbing since the tour of the east building, and she hadn't confronted the pain until now. It was definitely getting infected, judging by the slight green color and pus that encompassed the area, but Maya was too afraid to go back to the medical room alone. If that medical assistant wouldn't have been so cocky and rough with her, maybe she would've taken her time to do the stitches better.

So many thoughts were racing through Maya's mind. What kind of people were running this place? And what kind of medical staff had they recruited? She found a way to tie the shirt across her knee to maintain the pressure throughout the night. After what seemed like an eternity of rearranging her position, she finally felt comfortable enough to let the darkness consume her.

Maya dreamed that she and Caleb were running through the woods together during snowfall after successfully escaping the guards. Dreams are dreams, and they only reside as fantasies. Fantasies that do not come true.

Chapter 15
The First Day

The following morning, Eva woke up Maya at sunrise.

"I'm sorry." She whispered, "I thought you'd want to shower and get ready before breakfast."

The sun was peeking through the glass window panes as Maya rubbed the sleep from her eyes.

"Thank you." She mumbled in a tired voice. Eva was thoughtful. Without her, Maya probably would have missed breakfast. Maya grabbed a towel, uniform, and undergarments and followed the girls to the public showers. Only a couple of others had the same idea as Eva, it seemed.

After undressing and stepping into a shower, Maya realized the public showers were very... public. The girls and guys' showers were separated by a measly wall that was probably shorter than most of the guys. This annoyed Maya, especially after remembering Miles probably made an inappropriate comment about her. Caleb was going to be upset, too.

As soon as Maya turned the shower head-on, she cursed aloud.

"What's wrong?" Danielle and Faye turned to her with concerned looks.

Maya's knee was getting worse. Her knee seemed to be inflamed and swelling along with the different shades of greens and yellows that surrounded the stitches.

"Sorry, I just stubbed my toe." Maya angled her knee away from the pressure of the water.

She quickly rinsed her body with a soap bar and washed her hair with the shampoo and conditioner that was given to them in their hygiene packs. Maya wished she could stay under the running water forever. She was refreshed and the cleanest she'd felt in a while.

She stepped out of the shower after wringing out her hair and quickly covered herself with a towel while heading over to the changing area. She got dressed, being mindful of her knee, and braided her damp hair. The girls all brushed their teeth and headed back to their room since they still had an hour to spare until breakfast.

Noticing that Caleb hadn't been at the bathrooms or showers, Maya knocked three times in room 110 as they passed by. She didn't want him to be late for breakfast, or he'd have to starve until lunch. After yesterday's dinner, she was hopeful for a wholesome breakfast.

Her knee had swelled so much that with each step, she began to feel herself limping. As much as she regretted to admit it, she needed to see the doctor today. She made a mental note to specifically go through Isabella, in the case that it may help her discover something about her. The girls settled back into their room and put their dirty clothes in the laundry basket that was labeled by their room number. By now, the sun had settled.

Maya wondered how long it would stay out today, given the bleak midwinter they were in. She fixed her bed, not knowing if they would have room checks, and advised the others to do the same. The room had the same white walls and white tiles that the outside hall contained. It didn't feel homely at all and seemed more like a jail cell. The furniture that decorated the room were all of some sort of silver metal, matching the theme of the rest of the buildings.

"How long had you guys been at the shelter before we got picked up?" Maya was curious. It was frustrating to her that even though everyone had been kidnapped from the same shelter, no one really knew each other. Maybe that's why they hadn't become a united front. It's easier to fend for yourself when you have no emotional ties to anyone.

"About one month," Danielle spoke on hers and Eva's behalf. They were friends before going into the shelter like Caleb and Maya. Maya remembered seeing them around when she and Caleb first arrived.

"I was there for two weeks," Maya admitted. She was sitting sprawled out on the cold tile with her left leg extended. Her knee was so stiff that it had become difficult to bend. She didn't know how much longer she could go walking on it, but she was already dreading a visit to the medical wing.

"I guess I was the unluckiest." Faye sighed and ran her freckled fingers through her crimson hair. "That was my first day." Maya and the girls gasped. She really was unlucky. People are always going from and coming in shelters, but to have shown up on that specific day... Maya didn't know how Faye contained her anger.

Before they knew it, the clock struck 8 am, and the four girls gathered themselves to head upstairs. In the hallway, Maya reconnected with Caleb and noticed that he was able to shower. His wavy brunette hair was still damp, and he was in a fresh gray uniform that was a little too tight for his muscular arms.

"Did you hear my knocks?" She asked him curiously as she approached him.

"You might have to do that every morning." He spoke honestly and gratefully. He had always been difficult to wake up. They all began crowding up the narrow staircases.

"Hey, Mayhem. Thanks for the wakeup call." Miles winked at Maya from his position next to none other than Derek, who was a couple of stairs ahead of Maya and Caleb.

How bold, Maya thought. Was one black eye not enough?

Maya felt Caleb try to lurch forward and quickly grabbed his arm to hold him back. "Caleb, it's harmless," she hissed quietly in his ear to not draw attention to them.

Everyone finally filed into the dining hall. Maya could smell scents of cinnamon, maple syrup, and fruits. The aroma was intoxicating to all the shelter kids. She was surprised she could still even recognize the scents. Maya and Caleb found their way to their seats from the previous dinner, and it took an immense effort for her to hide her limp from everyone but specifically Caleb. She winced in pain with every step she took.

Another silver tray was presented to them, but this one contained French toast, an assortment of fruits, and scrambled eggs. Maya and Caleb's eyes bulged. They hadn't seen food like this in years, let alone having the opportunity to devour it.

"How's your knee?" Caleb asked between bites of French toast doused in maple syrup. Maya knew this question would come, and she had no other option except to lie. She wasn't ready to go in yet. She hadn't seen Isabella this morning.

"Better." She forced a smile to look more convincing. "I'll try to get it looked at soon," she added for extra reassurance.

This answer pleased Caleb.

They finished their breakfast together with the anticipation of what the day held for them. They would be beginning their classes today and weren't sure how to feel about it. Maya and Caleb both missed a couple of years of high school after escaping their last foster home, but they both had natural strengths when it came to education. Caleb was the type of student who didn't need to study to get an A on an exam, as school just came naturally to him. Maya, on the other hand, couldn't put down a math problem until she answered it correctly and understood how it was solved. Both kept up with their studies by reading random books and textbooks they found in shelters, and various bookstores they would sit in.

Today, their first class of the day was math. Maya was still curious to see how they would manage to teach to different age groups the same type of math course, but assuming that many of them had been in and out of shelters for so long, they all might as well be at the same educational level, which would be a basic one.

The clock struck 9 am, and everyone began filing out of the dining hall while cramming the last bit of their breakfast into their stomachs. It was almost as if the food was too good to be true, and no one could bear the thought of wasting any of it. Maya had a slight suspicion that it wouldn't stay this scrumptious for long. Mandala was still in the process of gaining everyone's trust, and the food was a genius way to do so. Give a bunch of starved homeless kids a place to live and delicious food, and they'll do almost anything. The children blindly followed one another to the mathematics classroom in anticipation. For some, eagerness was displayed across their faces at the chance to learn. For most of the older bunch, dread overcame them from the memories of past high school experiences.

Maya and Caleb, on the other hand, were conflicted. However, curiosity was still at its peak in their minds. As they made their way to the classroom, Maya hobbled a little behind Caleb, out of his view. It took an immense effort not to collapse in pain as they made their way through the hall, but she was determined to use her injury as a way to discover more about the place.

Upon entering, the classroom was set up in a lecture hall fashion to seat the near eighty people comfortably. Maya and Caleb found seats in the corner of the room closest to the door. At the front of the classroom stood a whiteboard that consumed the entire front wall, along with a guard and someone who appeared to be their professor. The man seemed to be in his mid-60s and had silver hair overtaking his previous head of black hair. He wore gray dress pants and a gray suit jacket, which was interesting to Maya. She had noticed that those with higher positions weren't limited to the bland gray uniform, so seeing their professor attempting to blend in sparked a whole new set of ideas in her already electric mind. Once warm bodies filled all the seats, the professor turned on his headset.

"Good morning, class. It's good to see so many new and bright faces. My name is Dr. Gordon. I hope you have all settled in nicely. Today, we will be brushing up on some simple algebra." It was weird to Maya how this manufactured classroom in this manufactured building in the middle of nowhere seemed to mimic an actual, realistic school so precisely. They still had no idea why they had been brought to Mandala, but there was a sense of comfort sitting in that classroom surrounded by peers and a warming face at the front of the room, minus the guard.

Dr. Gordon wrote his name with a black expo marker on the whiteboard. Out of all the futuristic furnishings around the building, this room seemed to be the only accurate representation of the outside world. The thoughts running around Maya's brain made the class fly by. Images of solving for "x" on the whiteboard flashed before her eyes as the class ended. Dr. Gordon didn't call on anyone for answers, didn't force anyone to go to the whiteboard to solve a problem, and it even looked like his guard was falling asleep. She was too distracted by her own questions about Mandala to show the professor any attention.

Before she knew it, Dr. Gordon was writing chemistry on the board and drawing figures of test tubes and graduated cylinders with symbols of the elements to decorate them. As much as she wanted to pay attention to what appeared to be a sweet old man, her mind wandered to other places as she examined her surroundings. The guard was definitely snoozing now, despite the empty coffee cup that sat on the small desk in front of him. Weird. Dr. Gordon took one look at the sleeping guard and began erasing the board in a hurry.

"Alright class, I have you for an hour and a half before you're released to lunch, so I am going to teach you how to make a bomb with household essentials." The class all looked around at each other with confused faces. "Caleb." Maya nudged his arm to wake him from his daydream.

"I think he drugged the guard."

Without the professor confirming that he was on their side, everyone could just tell. Students began ripping pages from the new notebooks they had been presented with and finally uncapped their pens. Maya had goosebumps raise up and down the lengths of both her arms. She didn't know if this was all a ploy, but she had to go with the hope that the professor was genuine. Maybe she would learn something that could potentially save her life in this place.

The professor was talking and writing on the board at a rapid pace because he knew how imperative it was to get all of this information out. He didn't even stop to consider the fact that some of the kids might be considering playing for the other team now. Maybe he just didn't care.

"Making a pipe bomb is highly effective because the small airway allows for increased pressure, creating a bigger explosion depending on the explosive material you pack it with, such as a chlorate mixture..." He was back to drawing figures of test tubes and graduated cylinders on the board, showing examples of explosive mixtures and various amounts of liquids that should be used.

"And always, wear gloves."

And with that, the board was quickly erased without asking if the class had been sure to write it down. The guard began rubbing the sleep from his eyes, as the clock struck 1 pm for lunch. There was no time for questions. Just a goodbye, and "I'll see you tomorrow in class."

It had left everyone in a shocked and confused state, but no one knew what even to ask each other.

They all closed their notebooks and shoved it into their bags as if their lives may depend on it. Which they probably did.

Maya and Caleb followed the others to the dining hall with a newer and hungrier appetite. They might be able to get out of here after all.

In the dining hall, Maya finally found Isabella, who she had grown increasingly impatient for. Her knee was now swelling to the size of a balloon, and she could feel the fluid inside that inflamed it. She decided to quickly scarf down her lunch, which consisted of grilled chicken, rice, and an assortment of colorful vegetables. As much as she wished she could savor each bite, her knee needed more attention.

"Caleb, I'm going to talk to Isabella about going to the medical wing before humanities," she said as she washed down her last bite with a swig of water.

"Finally. I'll be here," he assured her. Caleb had a look of relief on his face.

Maya found her way to Isabella, who was sitting alone at the end of one of the long white tables. Her food looked like it had barely been touched, which Maya couldn't bear the thought of since the chicken and vegetables had made her discover new taste buds she never even knew she had.

"Isabella, can you please take me to the medical wing?" Maya was pleading. She didn't know how much longer she could fight back the tears of pain.

Isabella looked up at her with unslept eyes and messy hair. A concerned look drew on her face. "Of course, what's the matter?" She immediately rose from her seat and began leading Maya out of the dining hall, as if that was the excuse she had been waiting for to leave. As soon as she noticed Maya's limp, she asked to see her leg. Maya gently lifted her pant leg once they were out of sight and hidden on the back stairwell leading them downstairs. "I got a gash on my first day here, and they stitched it up, but I think it's infected." Her knee had swelled so large that the stitches appeared to be pulling and ready to rip at the seams.

Isabella gasped at the sight of her now-green knee. "Come with me."

She grabbed Maya by the arm and took the majority of her weight, as she swiftly guided her down the stairs and across the outdoor walkway to the west building. The frigid winter hadn't faltered, and a new set of snow covered the ground. There was no sun to admire, just dead trees in the distance.

"Why did you wait this long?" Isabella asked in an anger-filled tone.

This was the opportunity Maya had been waiting for.

"I don't really feel comfortable here and didn't know what to do. I obviously don't trust the medical staff, especially as they weren't able to properly give me five stitches. Are they even certified?" Maya was ready to go on a rampage with accusations, but she needed to maintain herself until she got feedback from Isabella, who sighed knowingly. "We'll have the doctor take a look at it. The medical staff isn't here to hurt you," she avoided eye contact as she used her ID card to grant them entrance to the west building. She sounded like a robot. Maya's trust hadn't been earned yet. She led Maya into the same room she had been examined in on the first day at Mandala. Today, the room was quieter. The same medical staff was present, but they seemed to be working on their own labs and projects. There were benches with microscopes and petri dishes filled with unknowns.

The medical assistant who had stitched up Maya's knee instantly recognized her and had a regrettable look on her face. Her stubbornness got the best of her, and she knew she had sutured too quickly. Isabella took Maya straight to the doctor, who was running the show on opening day. "Dr. Salvi, I think you should take a look at her knee." Dr. Salvi had a fiery aura. She was small but mighty. Extremely intelligent but maybe too much for her own good.

She tied her curly blonde hair up and out of her face and proceeded to lift Maya's pant leg. "This is severely infected," she placed her hands on her hips as she did some calculations in her brain. "I need a syringe!" Dr. Salvi called out, and immediately, medical assistants were roaming around in a hurry.

Gloves and a syringe were quickly in her hands, and she knelt down to be eye level with Maya's knee. "There's way too much fluid in here. I'm going to remove it, re-suture the wound, and put you on antibiotics and a pain killer. In the meantime, while it heals, I need you to ice it and elevate it whenever you're in your room." she spoke as she worked. Maybe a form of distraction to patients? She stuck the needle into Maya's knee and pulled back the fluid using the syringe.

"If your knee swells like this again, make sure to come back immediately. This fluid needs to be flushed."

A mumbled "Okay" was all Maya could muster, as she fought back the sickening feeling of seeing the needle in her knee.

Without faltering her work or looking up, Dr. Salvi called out to her staff. "Which one of you sutured her?" Maya looked out at them with a feeling of regret. Even though she was angry at the medical assistant, she didn't necessarily want her to get punished. It seemed like days flew by until the culprit finally owned up to her poorly performed work.

"It was me, Dr. Salvi." The medical assistant with wide eyes spoke sheepishly.

"Anna?" Dr. Salvi recognized her voice, still refusing to look up from her work.

"Yes, ma'am. There were just so many of them that day that I guess I was rushing and-" She attempted to explain herself, but Dr. Salvi cut her off.

"This work is horrendous. You will be switching to the clothing sector. Maybe your poor excuse for stitches will be required in their sewing department," she spoke harshly, and Maya could have sworn spit was hitting her leg.

"Yes, ma'am." Anna's voice was shaky from a quivering lip. She held back her tears as she packed up her few items and quickly left the room.

Maya felt an overwhelming sense of guilt. She knew it wasn't her fault, but she cursed her immune system for letting an infection spread and causing this domino effect. She didn't need another enemy here.

Maya was at a loss for words as Dr. Salvi finished tending to her knee. She gave Maya two pills, an antibiotic and a painkiller, and watched her wash it down with water. She wrapped her knee and sent Maya and Isabella on their way.

Maya felt instant relief as she stepped off of the table onto her leg. Removing the fluid took much of the soreness away, and although she still felt pain, it was much better than before. Isabella used her key card and led them back to the east building.

"Why did she kick her out like that? It was obviously a mistake," Maya interrupted their silence.

"You can't make mistakes here. If there are mistakes, there are risks. You could've had your leg amputated if you waited any longer, and the infection had spread." Isabella spoke sternly and never met Maya's eyes.

Maya wasn't getting any of the answers she needed. Isabella was behaving like a brick wall.

"When were you brought here?" Maya chose a risky choice of words purposefully. Maybe if she assumed Maya's suspicion, she would give in to it. Isabella gave her a curious look and opened her mouth to respond, but Maya asked too late. Isabella was saved by the chime of the clock, striking 2 pm overhead as they entered the upstairs hallway of the east building.

It was time for humanities.

Chapter 16
Humanities

Maya waited outside of the dining hall until Caleb entered so they could go to humanities together. Since their table was in the back corner of the dining hall, he was the last to walk out.

"How did it go?" He asked as soon as he laid eyes on Maya, his eyebrows furrowed in worry.

"It went fine, the doctor redid my stitches, but she kicked out the medical assistant who originally did them." Maya looked at his face for a reaction.

"That's kind of harsh. Maybe she had it coming." He tried to cheer up Maya after seeing how upset she looked. They shrugged their shoulders and entered the humanities classroom at the end of the hall. Since they were the last to join, the only seats that remained were in the front. This classroom was set up much differently. Five rows of silver metal chairs and tables wrapped around the center of the room in circles. Some sort of 3D holographic screen was being projected and consumed the entire center of the room from floor to ceiling.

A new professor and guard stood in the center.

The professor was a middle-aged man with jet black hair and dark eyes to match. He had a muscular build, the ex-military type. He was frowning, and his demeanor seemed to be a polar opposite of their previous professor.

"Good afternoon, everyone. This will be your humanities class. As stated before, you will probably be here a while. No one leaves until the last person stops crying." Maya and Caleb immediately made eye contact, and everyone began chatting to each other in confusion.

"Silence!" He demanded. "The faster we begin, hopefully, the faster this will end." He took a sip from a mug that reeked of alcohol from where Maya and Caleb were sitting.

"Today's video is on a 10-year-old boy committing suicide. We'll start you off light," he began pressing buttons from a remote, and the holographic screen lit up and flickered until it clearly displayed a young boy in an office. The projection was so real that it felt like they were in the room with him. The technology was life-like, and the dimensions were accurate to real objects and people.

"What movie is this from?" Derek's voice was heard from the back of the room.

"This isn't a movie. This is live video." The unnamed professor had a horrific smirk to his face as he took another swig from his mug. Maya was in shock. If this was a live video, why were they even allowing it to happen?

"Make him stop! Tell him not to do it! Do something!" Maya was screaming hysterically. Her head was spinning, and she could not roam her mind quick enough for any good reason as to why they were at Mandala, and why they were being forced to watch a child kill himself. People began to join in with her cries, but with one swift head nod to the guard, their yells were quickly silenced by his baton.

Maya grabbed Caleb's arm and squeezed. She was going to be here a while. During their shouts to end what was going on, the boy had begun to make some leeway in his potential death. He was pacing around an office while searching for something.

Pills?

A rope?

A knife?

A *gun.* He found a gun under the desk. Presumably, his father's gun that had been so carelessly placed underneath his desk. The classroom filled with a symphony of tears and yells, leading to more strikes by the baton. There was no sympathy. Maya dug her nails into Caleb's arm as tears streamed down her face.

"Maya, close your eyes." He whispered to her in a soothing tone. Maya obeyed and slowly released her grip on Caleb. Suddenly, Maya felt Caleb rise from his chair as the sound of a baton smacked the table next to Maya.

"Your eyes must remain open!" The professor echoed throughout the classroom. The guard faced Maya to strike her, but Caleb positioned himself in front of her and had to take the blow himself as a consequence of such risky behavior. Maya winced as the baton struck Caleb's arm with such intensity, she swore she could hear a bone crack. Maya's cries were near hysterical now as she held onto Caleb when the gunshot went off. The little boy couldn't handle the recoil of the gun, causing the bullet to only penetrate the right side of his face instead of through the mouth to the brain as he had planned. This caused his blood-curdling screams, and crimson blood to gush from his cheek. Everyone in the classroom was sobbing at this point and screaming to end it. Guards filtered in and lined the back walls of the room prepared to strike. Maya wanted nothing more than for the video to end. Why were no adults rushing into the room to help him? Could no one but them hear his cries?

The little boy struggled to pick the gun back up to finish the job. He was in too much pain and covered in a pool of blood. After fumbling with the gun for what seemed like decades, he finally got a steady hold of it. Was it terrible to want him to finish it so that he wasn't in pain anymore? It was evident that no one would be coming to help him, right? Wrong.

Just as the second bullet rang out, causing the room to jump in fear, a woman came bursting through the room half a second too late. The bullet was successful in ending the poor boy's life, creating a mural of blood splatters on the white wall behind him. His body slumped forward, and his hand still held the gun.

"Jacob! Jacob! No Jacob! What did you do? What did you do?" The woman that seemed to be his mother was in a ball on the floor, embracing her son. Her tears mixed with the blood that covered his body, his face mangled and unrecognizable.

Everyone in the classroom was weeping, aside from the professor and guards. Maya was wondering how they could be so heartless and inhuman. The hologram in the center of the room froze on the image of the mother holding the son. However, the cries from Maya and her classmates did not cease. No one had the energy to question what was just witnessed. The extra guards left the room as they were no longer required.

After a full hour of what seemed to be pure exhaustion of emptying tear ducts, the students were released on the condition that everyone had stopped wailing. The students left the room with bloodshot, puffy eyes, and a new feeling of fatigue that overtook their bodies. Together, and in an orchestration of whimpers and sniffles, they headed downstairs back to their dorms. The clock struck 4 pm, which wasn't a horrible time to be done for the day, but the professor's words echoed in Maya's head, "We'll start you off light."

It would only be getting worse from here.

Once they reached the first floor, Maya made eye contact with Isabella, who was returning to her own room. A new sense of rage filled Maya. She wanted answers, and she wanted them tonight. Caleb followed Maya as she pushed through the crowd of everyone swarming the halls, trying to relocate their rooms to most likely cry themselves to sleep, while she attempted to track down Isabella. Isabella had seen the fury that consumed Maya's swollen green eyes and hurried at a faster pace toward her room. Maya was faster.

She slid in through the door just as Isabella was making an attempt to close it behind herself. Caleb had not been so lucky to make it inside but waited patiently outside as if he was Maya's bodyguard. Isabella faced Maya with her own set of swollen eyes, but fear encompassed her freckled face.

"I want to know precisely what is going on here, and I want to know why we were forced to witness that." Maya was seething. She didn't care if this girl was also brought here against her will. She was tired of being in the dark. Isabella put her hands up in a defensive manner as if Maya might attack. "I'll tell you what I know, just please be quiet." Maya didn't know if Isabella was talking about the paper-thin walls or potential bugs in the room, but she didn't have the time to consider the possibilities either. Tears stained both the girls' faces. "I was brought here a year ago.

They kidnapped me one night when I was leaving my college campus to go home," she sniffled back a tear that was trying to escape. Her voice sounded hoarse. "They told me that they were doing this to better society and that I was going to become a part of a greater picture. Mandala warned me that they were bringing children, and I tried so many times to escape so that I could warn the police, but their system is too difficult to beat. There are guards everywhere all the time," she rubbed her eyes and gathered herself.

"Did they tell you what they're doing with us here? What are we going to do that's going to help society?" Maya asked in a softer voice now. She didn't want to direct her anger toward Isabella anymore. She was a victim just as much as the rest of them, but she had endured this torture much longer. "All I know is that they are trying to desensitize all of us. They want to use us for some greater purpose, and to do it, we can't have emotions any longer. I don't know what their plan is, but I'm supposed to keep all of you in check so that their plan doesn't falter. I can't even be seen with you, or they'll start to get suspicious."

Desensitize? No longer have emotions?

Maya didn't know how to process any of this. The desensitization explained their humanities class, but it didn't explain mathematics, science, economics, and, more importantly, it didn't explain *why*. Her head was pounding with this new information, and she felt dehydrated from crying out all of the water in her body. Without another word, she exited Isabella's room to a worried-looking Caleb.

"Desensitized?" he asked with furrowed brows. He heard.

The pair walked to the common bathrooms together to wash their faces and give themselves time to think of what to do.

"Maybe Dr. Gordon will have a better idea of what's going on," Caleb suggested in a whisper while the faucet ran. They couldn't risk anything anymore. If they were going to get to the bottom of this, they couldn't get caught. "Okay, we can't rush this. We have to wait till the time and opportunity are right to find out more. We have to do this right." Maya was more determined than ever after witnessing that innocent little boy kill himself. She would not willingly give herself to this company, no matter what their purpose was. They also needed to be careful around their peers. People were still transitioning over to Mandala's side, in the hope for their own survival. This needed to stay between Maya, Caleb, and Isabella for now.

"I might just be paranoid, but what if Dr. Gordon is actually on Mandala's side, and it's a ploy to filter out the traitors?" Anything was possible at this point. Caleb raised his eyebrows in consideration. "We're going to have to wait this out a little."

They both sighed, not knowing how much more of the humanities class they could manage. Derek and Miles sauntered into the bathroom, seemingly unfazed by the earlier tragedy. Maya couldn't tell if it was all a façade or if they really weren't affected by the video. Caleb immediately tensed in response to their presence.

"Quite a show you guys put on in there," Derek displayed a smirk of self-amusement. Maya and Caleb made it a point not to respond, but Derek didn't budge.

"As much as you guys don't want to admit it, we're on your side," he motioned to himself and Miles.

With clenched teeth, Maya faced him, "What side is that, Derek?" Maya knew to be cautious with Derek. He always had an ulterior motive that made her wary of telling him too much information.

"We want to escape." He whispered while checking around for any potential listeners. This caused Caleb to roll his eyes. "And how are we going to do that?" Maya and Caleb needed to play off their parts as clueless, but they were secretly open to ideas.

Derek disappeared into a bathroom stall, and after a grunt and sounds of metal clanking, he reappeared holding a small pipe.

"We can start with a bomb."

The four of them exited the bathrooms after having been there for a suspiciously long time and after removing a suspicious amount of pipes from various utilities in the bathroom. Although Maya felt uneasy being in Miles's presence, she felt comfort in knowing that nothing would happen while Caleb was there, and she also knew that a more significant matter was at hand. Maya and Caleb had to set their feelings aside for their own well-being. It was still well before 9 pm, so they had some time to be in each other's rooms and decided on going to Caleb and Miles's room.

The room was empty when they arrived, so they took their opportunity to talk and get to creating the bombs and discussing how to get an explosive chemical. Their room was identical to Maya's but, not surprisingly, messier. They all eventually agreed that the only way to get some sort of chemical would be in the medical wing that Maya had grown familiar with.

This project gave Maya something to focus on. It satisfied her craving to be doing something that would be aiding their plan to escape. Since they'd all arrived, she had felt useless in her attempts to find out more about Mandala, and how to put an end to his company.

Chapter 17
Mayhem

Days turned into weeks that turned into months of what seemed to be an eternity of heartache and pain that was endured in the humanities class. Winter snow eventually melted into spring blooms, but it went without admiration. The days turned into routines of occasionally witnessing the professor drug his guard in order to teach a vital survival tip, rarely being able to eat during meals anymore, struggling through humanities, and then sobbing themselves to sleep.

The food quality and quantity had diminished in response to everyone's nonexistent appetite. Humanities never became more bearable, but each person was slowly running out of tears to produce. Some students had even found access to the humanities professor's alcohol stash and couldn't get through the days without it.

Maya had developed a craving for the pain medications she had been on for her knee and was always in and out of the medical wing complaining of knee problems to get more. It enabled her to continually steal various chemicals, while also allowing her to get a steady supply of pills. Everyone wandered around like drugged zombies. The few who had decided to work with Mandala blended into the crowd effortlessly as moles. Every so often, someone who had been planning a potential escape ended up being a victim in the humanities class. Students were being tortured by the very hands of their own peers. Everyone was now being subjected to witnessing their own classmates be tortured on the holographic screen, as a part of their daily ritual.

Caleb had not sidelined his temper, however, and would punch anyone or anything that agitated him. His anger toward the company radiated, causing him to become a new target of suspicion to the moles. This put a restraint on Maya's original hopes for them to fly under the radar.

Their lives felt like constant nightmares.

One day, when Maya was in the medical wing for one of her regular check-ups, Dr. Salvi showed more interest in her blood type. "What blood type are you again?" Dr. Salvi casually asked as she examined Maya's knee.

"I never said." Maya raised her eyebrows and couldn't mask the perplexed look on her face. Why was Dr. Salvi asking her blood type? What would that help her with?

Maya knew her blood type to be AB-, a universal recipient. She didn't know what this information could mean to Dr. Salvi, so she decided to play clueless.

"I'm not sure what my blood type is. Maybe B positive?" Maya spoke in an unsure manner. Immediately, worst-case scenarios began playing in her mind. Had Dr. Salvi already tested her blood?

"I would like to do some blood and genetic testing on you." She stood from her knelt down position and walked over to a clipboard.

"Are you asking me or telling me?" Maya had grown bolder with the drugs she took routinely. She could tell that Dr. Salvi knew she had been milking her supply but probably allowed it to work in her favor at this very moment.

Dr. Salvi gave no verbal response except for a slight smirk that presented an obvious answer to Maya's question.

"What are you going to do to me?" Maya asked.

"I just want to alter certain gene expression. This same procedure has been done before on a baby. I'm sure you'll be fine. Don't worry, your DNA won't be changed at all." The doctor spoke with such ease that it almost seemed like a routine procedure to Maya in her drugged haze. Almost.

"What gene do you want to alter? What do you want to do to me?" Maya's forehead began to sweat from panic. She regretted all of her unnecessary visits to the medical wing now. She gave Dr. Salvi too much opportunity to plan this all out, and now she was the perfect guinea pig.

"It's not something to worry about. If anything, it benefits you. I just want to mimic the process of gene doping to increase your red blood cell count, which in turn will boost athletic performance." Her words were gibberish to Maya. She hadn't been in school long enough to understand genetics well. Dr. Salvi's spiel seemed promising to any clueless person, but not to Maya. This experiment was just another way to benefit Mandala's mission. "It could help with your knee, too," she added. They want me to become a mole, Maya thought. Why else would they want her athletic performance to increase?

Without consent, Dr. Salvi began taking vials of Maya's blood for further testing and even took a skin biopsy.

"How much blood do you need?" Maya asked from her frozen position. Her body was too weak to try and run away, and her fear of needles kept her immobile.

"One more tube. Almost done," the other staff in the room came one by one to collect the vials and immediately returned to their stations with petri dishes and microscopes.

"I'll see you soon, Maya." Dr. Salvi gave her a malicious smirk and then called for Isabella, who was waiting outside of the room. Ever since she picked up on Isabella and Maya's inseparability, she had ordered her to remain outside the room.

Isabella came to help Maya off of the table and quickly noticed the bandages on Maya's arms. She hid her confused expression and decided to wait until they left the medical wing to interrogate Maya.

Once safely out of the west building, she stopped Maya in her tracks.

"What did they do to you? Aren't they supposed to be monitoring your knee?" Isabella flipped Maya's arms to take a closer look at the bandages.

Maya had an annoyed response. All she wanted to do whenever she received her pills was to lay down and sulk, and at this particular visit, Dr. Salvi gave her none.

"She said she wants to alter my gene expression." Maya had air quotes around the word alter. She didn't have full faith that it was something that could be done.

"Epigenetics." Isabella gasped. Mandala hadn't done that in decades. Since the testing on the babies.

"We can't go back there," Isabella spoke sternly, as they continued their walk back to the dining hall.

"Um, yes, we can." Maya's voice was loud, "I need more pills. I'm running out." Maya was already becoming agitated. She had counted only two pills left from her bottle, which would only last her two days at most if she rationed them.

Isabella decided against arguing. She would have to talk with Caleb alone so they could detox her. Her mind was clouded, and she didn't have the same determined mindset as when she had first arrived. Genetic testing would take a heavy toll on her already exhausted body. Isabella made a mental note to catch Caleb at night while Maya was in the showers.

Maya's entire routine had changed as the days went on. She was no longer an early bird, ready to take on whatever Mandala brought to them each day. Instead, she preferred to sleep in for as long as possible and take her showers at night despite Caleb's concerns. Isabella dropped off Maya in the dining hall, and their day went about as usual.

Humanities came after lunch, then a quiet dinner, followed by the showers. This was when she found Caleb.

"Can I talk to you for a second?" She motioned for him to enter the 'Staff Only' room. Caleb obliged, and after checking that no one in the halls had been paying attention, he entered.

"Did Maya talk to you today about her visit t o the medical wing?"

Caleb ran a hand through his hair. Maya had been barely talking to him lately, and he had been on edge because of it.

He admitted to Isabella that he was entirely out of the loop with Maya ever since she'd been taking pills.

"We've got to get rid of her last bottle." They both agreed. "And we have to keep her from going to the medical wing again."

After their discussion, Caleb quickly made it to Maya's room before her and was greeted by Danielle, Eva, and Farah. When the moles started coming out, he and Maya had agreed that these girls were most likely not on Mandala's side, leaving Maya's room as their safe room. The girls had similar views as them but were too afraid to join their fight against the company.

"Where are her pills?" Caleb didn't have time to catch up with the girls. He needed to move quickly for Maya's own safety. He knew this was something he should have done a long time ago, but they both were grieving in different ways.

Danielle pointed at Maya's pillowcase and quickly went back into her bunkbed. She didn't want to be a part of the reason for Maya's forced detox. They had all grown up in shelters. They knew of the difficulties that were to come.

THE NEW BREED

Chapter 18
The Detox

The days that ensued were the epitome of hell. Caleb and Isabella were forcing Maya to detox herself, and they refused to let her go to the medical wing. Maya fluctuated between having chills and hot flashes. She was always seen drenched in sweat or wrapped in a blanket.

She was plagued with anxiety and insomnia, and her restlessness was apparent. Her symptoms began with shaking hands and cold sweats. Shortly after, she experienced a fever accompanied by severe dizziness. She begged and begged for Caleb and Isabella to take her to the medical wing for more pills. Maya could feel pain throughout her bones, causing her entire body to go weak.

After only two days of detoxing, she began vomiting and remained in the showers for the cold water. She became nearly unrecognizable to her peers. Everyone knew that the only way to help her was to allow her to endure the entire detoxification process. They couldn't give in to her demands, as miserable as it was to see her like that.

Dr. Gordon excused her from his classes, but she was never excused from humanities. Even on her worst days, she was forced to endure the trauma of the class. Caleb and Isabella were at her side persistently, despite Maya's hatred toward them for the detox. Maya began each day with a new sense of kindness toward them for the sole purpose of persuading them to get her more pills. Her affection never got her far, and the rest of the day would be spent screaming and attempting to hit Caleb and Isabella.

Caleb hated seeing her like this. In all their years of friendship, she had always been the rock - the consistent one of the pair. Maya had always been the one to help Caleb recover from a bad spot, and now that the scripts had flipped, he found himself struggling to play Maya's part.

Despite Isabella and Caleb's best efforts to hide the detox efforts from Dr. Salvi, she eventually found out through moles, and one day during lunch, paramedics came to collect Maya. Maya didn't struggle or cause a scene with the paramedics. It was what she had truly wanted. The medical wing contained the pills she needed, and if this was the way to get her there, so be it.

It was now easy for Dr. Salvi to have Maya in her reach by using her detox symptoms as an excusable reason to acquire her without any questions. Isabella and Caleb had no say in the matter, and Maya was taken away for three days.

Caleb was constantly stealing Isabella's staff key card and making his way to the west building to check up on Maya. His efforts never made it inside of the medical wing and were limited to seeing her through the door's glass window. He could only ever see that she was unconscious and strapped to a table with various tubes sticking out of her. Guards were getting tired of having to remove Caleb forcibly so forcibly, and on the third day of Maya's absence, Caleb was not permitted to leave his dorm room. He had his own personal guard watching him at all times.

The epigenetics was working at its prime and could not be messed with. Caleb had to be detained so that Mandala's experiment worked effectively. On the fourth day, Maya was finally released. She appeared at breakfast as if nothing had happened. She had no more withdrawal symptoms and seemed to have more energy than when they all had arrived at Mandala. Her dark under-eye circles were replaced with fresh, glowing skin. Her hair was washed and healthy, and she had a new stride to her step.

Isabella and Caleb were immediately at her side.

Before they could badger Maya with any questions, Maya immediately was struck with the guilt of her behavior during her drug detox. "I'm so sorry, guys. I didn't mean any of it. Please know that."

Isabella and Caleb gave no mind to her apologies. It wasn't necessary. Maya was their friend, and she was in desperate need of help. They did what had to be done and accepted the consequences.

"Are you okay? What did they do to you?" Caleb's fists were shaking, his veins stuck out from his neck in fear for Maya.

Maya was fully conscious now and able to answer Caleb and Isabella's questions. Mandala had visited her while on bed rest and explained what they had done to her, but he had still refrained from giving any reasoning.

"He told me they mimicked the drug Erythropoietin in my genes, which is used to increase athletic performance. I still don't know why they did it or why they picked me."

Maya's glassy eyes violently moved across the room. She still had a suspicion that Mandala wanted her to be used as a mole, and although she could feel the increase in energy her body now had, she had no intention of letting Mandala or Dr. Salvi know that their experiment worked. She had to be careful about who she talked around and made a mental note to appear tired after doing activities like climbing a flight of stairs.

She knew they'd be monitoring her through the cameras and needed to make sure she put on a good show. Maybe they were right. Perhaps this experiment could help her. But one thing was for sure. She would not be using her new power to help Mandala. In the following week, Maya was continually being pulled out of Dr. Gordon's class to do energy expending activities such as running.

Dr. Salvi and Mandala were taking their own notes on how well she was performing. Purposely, Maya never ran past a mile to show them that her energy had not improved. She would always stop short of breath after any of the workouts they required her to do. "What are you guys trying to do here? Make me a track athlete?" Maya had grown comfortable enough to be snappy even to Mandala.

She felt that she had permission for her agitation, given that they had altered her genes without Maya's consent. She was pretending to play along with their game, but she wasn't going to make it easy on them.

"This doesn't make any sense. Her recent blood work shows a major increase in red blood cell count." Dr. Salvi was frustrated. Maya was chosen for her ripe age of sixteen, where the research work supposedly had the highest chance of success. Maya was making her look bad in front of Mandala. No one's spot at this company was safe. Mandala always made it clear that everyone was expendable. If she failed to please him, she would end up like Anna or worse.

Mandala walked away in resentment. "Test her again," he called out as he walked off of the field. As soon as he was no longer in sight, Dr. Salvi approached Maya and gripped her arm tightly. "What exactly do you think you're doing here?" She seethed. "I know you can run longer than that." Maya could feel bruises forming on her tender arms. "I'm doing the best that I can." Maya gave an innocent yet convincing look as she pulled her arm away from Dr. Salvi's reach. "It was your job to make sure this worked.

Not mine." And with that, Maya took off back towards the east building to join her peers. She would never give them the satisfaction or allow them to use her for one of their missions.

Chapter 19
The Moles

The duration of Dr. Gordon's stay was surprising, given the number of moles that sat amongst the rest of the class. Some theorized that he was pitied because of his age. Therefore, his absence one day came as a shock to many.

Upon entering the classroom, Maya noticed Isabella at the whiteboard. Once everyone was seated, she began to speak, "Dr. Gordon is no longer with us. Until we find a replacement, I will be teaching you all." Isabella's shaky voice mimicked the nervousness that vibrated through her hands. The guard looked suspiciously alert today, with crossed arms and accusing eyes at all of the students. He knew what the professor had been doing.

After what seemed to be a lesson that lasted an eternity, the students were released for lunch, which had now been limited to water, bread, and slop due to the students' refusals to eat. The dining hall, once filled with whispers and chatter, was now uncomfortably silent, while everyone picked at their food and awaited the most disturbing part of their day.

Every part of their day was moving in slow motion. The sound of the clock dictated all their movements and decisions as if they had no control over their bodies. The students obeyed the 2 pm ring that echoed through the building and made their way to the dreaded humanities classroom. As they took their seats, they noticed Mandala standing at the center of the room with a joy-filled grin.

Mandala didn't make appearances often, leaving all of the busy work and preparation for his staff. He only ever surfaced for important announcements that he wanted full credit for. He had proven himself to be an egotistical narcissist. "Hello everyone," his voice boomed and bounced off of the walls of the room. "The majority of you are responding quite well to the desensitization process and have proven yourselves to be ready to go into the field."

Maya escaped her drugged daze to process what he was saying. To go into the field? Was he sending people out of here? Mandala was a smart man. He was fulfilling the fantasies of children, wanting to become spies. He altered the reality of his objectives to persuade them to execute his plans voluntarily.

He proceeded by calling out ten names of those whom he deemed qualified and officially desensitized. Neither Maya nor Caleb's names were called. It was obvious that they had an inherent need to rebel. Included in the ten names was Derek's. After enduring so many of the humanities classes, Mandala broke him. He didn't consult Maya and Caleb anymore with the hopes of an escape plan. He joined the others in becoming puppet-like and giving in to all of Mandala's demands.

After calling out all the names, Mandala demanded the class to clap in the appraisal at their accomplishment. He explained that he would talk to them in private at dinner time and inform them of their missions. The most that Maya could understand from all of this was that they would now be moles in the real world. She made a mental note to talk to Isabella later. Mandala left after the announcement, and the professor began the day's video on a woman being set on fire.

She wasn't surprised that her own name hadn't been called. It made sense that the experiment performed on her would have been for this specific opportunity, but Maya had done too well of a job to let him think that it worked. He knew he would be risking too much by sending her out in the real world. Maya still had a mouth on her, and let him know it every chance she got. Humanities and dinner went by in a blur. The ten students who were called away by Mandala were taken elsewhere for their private dinner. This allowed Maya to talk to Isabella with fewer moles around to know. On the way back to the dorms after dinner, Maya followed Isabella to her room while Caleb waited patiently outside to make sure that no one was listening.

"What is Mandala sending them out to do?" Maya got straight to it. She thought that by being able to keep watch over everyone under one roof, they were somewhat safe. But now, everyone had different objectives, and Mandala was making it more challenging to watch out for their safety.

Isabella had her permanent worried look sprawled across her face. The expression never changed - wide eyes, creased forehead, and shaky hands. "Mandala wants to restart our society. He's using all of us to create a new breed. He says that we are emotionless so that we can go out and do his assignments. He's sending people into the field to attack large corporations and political figures so he can take over." Over the course of time that Isabella and Maya had come to know each other, Isabella finally became comfortable in confiding valuable information to Maya. Knowing that someone else was on her side put her at ease.

"And how exactly are they going to '*attack*'?" Air quotes surrounded the word attack when Maya spoke. Her head was spinning, and she was worried about what Isabella's response might be.

"Kill."

Chapter 20
Caleb

The following day, the ten people that Mandala had called upon were gone. He moved efficiently to accomplish his goals and had probably grown impatient with how long it had taken them to become desensitized. Everyone else continued their routines and obeyed each ding of the clock to execute their next move with precision.

The ensuing days mimicked each other entirely. Nothing out of the ordinary occurred. Isabella continued to teach mathematics, science, and economics but gave no informative survival tips out of fear from Mandala as well as the guard that kept a watchful eye.

Each move that Maya and Caleb wanted to make required patience, but the longer they waited, the more pain they had to suffer in the humanities class. Eventually, one day something peculiar happened. During their lunch hour before the humanities class, an announcement was made over the intercom by Mandala.

"A randomized search will be made in each of your rooms during lunch today. New information has surfaced that a classmate is putting your lives at risk. Carry on and enjoy your lunch."

Instantaneous fear fell over Caleb's face. The homemade bombs that they had prepared were hiding under his bunk wrapped in clothes. Maya searched the room for Miles, who had the same look of shock. Had Derek ratted them out before leaving? There was no way Miles and Caleb's other roommate had known, and as much as Maya enjoyed the company of her own roommates, she never confided that information to them. So much had happened since they made the bombs that Maya almost forgot they still had them.

Maya grabbed Caleb's hand in a failed attempt to calm him. "Maybe it's about someone else. Let's not get ahead of ourselves and worry for no reason." Maya knew that this false sense of hope was too good to be true. They sat in silence and moved their food around with a fork as they awaited the results of the search. Two minutes before lunch ended, an alarm blared from throughout the building.

"What's going on?" Maya wasn't sure if the alarm was because of the dorm search or something more concerning.

While the alarm continued to blare, guards entered the dining room and laid their eyes on Caleb as they marched toward him.

"No, no, no!" Maya stood in front of Caleb as they approached.

"He didn't do anything," she pleaded.

With one swift smack of a baton, Maya was out of the way. Three different guards grabbed Caleb simultaneously. He was kicking and cursing as they dragged him out in front of his peers, but the guards easily overpowered him. Caleb had lost much of his strength due to the loss of appetite that had occurred months ago.

The guards disappeared as quickly as they had entered, and the clock struck 2 pm, never faltering. As if nothing had happened, the students made their way to humanities. Isabella ran to Maya and helped her stand and recover after the baton. Maya was shivering from fear. "What are they going to do to him?" her lip quivered with horrific thoughts. Isabella had no comforting answers to give, as she led her down the hall along with the rest of the students.

When Maya entered the classroom, she made her way to her seat at the front next to Caleb's empty chair. Her skin was hot with rage.

She sat in silence, waiting for the professor to enter who was usually never late. Ten minutes went by before he arrived.

"Good afternoon, class. Sorry for the wait. It took a little longer to prepare today's video." There was an odd sense of glee that consumed him.

"Today, we will be watching a video on torture. As usual, we will not be leaving until the last student stops crying. Expect today to be quite a long day." Goosebumps formed all over Maya's arms. The professor stared at her as he made his last statement. Something was very wrong.

Today's video was featuring Caleb.

PART THREE

Chapter 21
The Arrival

Once we arrived at the camp, we were stunned to see its magnitude. Two glass buildings towered over us, connected by a walkway littered with guards. The guards were pacing around in white padded suits and held large guns. We weren't able to see their eyes as they were shielded by black sunglasses, making us more cautious about whether or not we could be seen.

"They've upgraded," James commented after examining our surroundings. He looked on edge. We were bringing him back to the place that brought him the most pain.

"Would we still be able to get in as we planned?" I faced James hoping for an easy solution, but the look on his face suggested otherwise.

"Yeah, it is possible. I've just got to think of something." He answered while looking around like he was scanning for a flaw in the structure.

Our main concern was avoiding the surrounding cameras that rotated with every movement that was detected outside of the camp. The four of us were crouched down in a densely wooded area, feeling naked without the safety of the Firebird. I hated abandoning it at the front of the forest since it left us with a very complicated exit strategy.

As we sat crouched, contemplating our next move, I felt hopeless in what we were about to do. Was this really going to work? Would we be spotted immediately and shot on sight? Many more possibilities were indicating this entire journey would go south, as opposed to working in our favor. I knew we had gone over the plan over and over again, but we had certainly not expected the company to be this large. James had told us it consisted of two buildings.

The mistake we had made was not thinking that the company would have expanded. Our plan could work, but I doubted its efficiency. The only thing on my mind pushing me forward was the image of my mom. This was a cause worth dying for. It would just mean so much more to accomplish what we came here to do successfully. Once I took myself out of my thoughts, I confronted the others. "We can't stay here. We need to put the plan in motion." I could see the wariness in their eyes as they nodded in agreement.

"Over there," Zeke pointed at the building to the right of us. "That's where we have to enter."

Zeke had analyzed the area and noticed a corner from the east tower that seemed to be a blind spot from all of the cameras except one. We would have to somehow disable or block that camera to make it into the building successfully. The problem, however, was that the camera was located outside the second floor, meaning we wouldn't be able to reach it fast enough to disable.

"There's no way we'd be able to disable it before they spot us," Amy concluded. She was the last addition to our group, and I had come to like her in the past few days. She was more on the sassy side, but she had a positive outlook on life, which came in handy when everything seemed gloomy.

My mind was doing calculations of all the entryways and the numbers of cameras. The four of us sat together, working out different possibilities and had the looming reminder that with every second, we were wasting precious time. We still had no idea about what Mandala was doing in the present day, which made our journey much more time-sensitive.

"What about the side of the west building?" I squinted, but we were too far away for me to notice any cameras.

"Guard on the roof and two cameras facing that way." Zeke's response was immediate. He had analyzed the camp in depth. It was good that we had him on the team, and I realized that I desperately needed glasses.

The heavily guarded camp left us with one option and one option only.

The company knew James. He was one of their lead experimenters. A title he no longer takes pride in. Although James escaped the company and has been on the run ever since we assumed or rather hoped that it would be more likely that they'd take him into questioning as opposed to shooting him on sight.

Allowing James to do this meant that we were sacrificing a lot. The person that had been leading the group would now no longer be in contact with us, forcing three experimentees to fend for ourselves. I was also sacrificing my uncle, who I had just reunited with after several years.

After too much time went by, I sighed. I knew what had to be done.

James had to be our distraction.

"Are you sure you're willing to do this?" I turned to James as he stood up and brushed the dirt off of his pants.

"We're doing this for Felicity," he reminded me. He looked at me with a tinge of regret in his eyes. We had barely caught up during this entire journey. We were still missing a five-year gap in each other's lives, and now, there was the possibility that we would never be able to reconnect.

My heart felt heavy, but we all knew this was the only way. None of the calculations I worked out in my head offered us any viable options. It was this moment of now or never.

"Okay, the camp is surrounded by tall fences and barbed wire. That gate is your only entrance when they open it for me." James pointed directly ahead of us to a large metal gate.

Looking back at me one last time, he whispered, "You follow on with the rest of the plan. Hopefully, I'll see you soon." I could not afford to reply to him verbally because I was afraid my emotions might get the best of me. All I could do was nod. We watched in anticipation as he trudged down to the grassy field, arms in the air to show that he was surrendering. The gate made a clanking sound and slowly opened. Shouts could be heard from the guards at the walkway, and suddenly, gunfire along with a blaring alarm.

We watched in horror as a bullet struck James' right shoulder. I wanted to let out a cry, but Zeke covered my eyes and mouth to prevent me from reacting more. It was more important to go unnoticed.

I expected to hear more shots ring out, but suddenly it went quiet. We could only hear the sounds of birds chirping above us. I forced myself out of Zeke's shoulder and looked onto the field. James was holding his shoulder and, in a crippled shout, yelled: "It's James, experimenter 528611!"

I assumed the numbers were a form of identification.

The guards jumped from over the walkway to a ten-foot drop and sprinted toward James. It appeared that they recognized him and suddenly forced his hands into handcuffs, causing him to scream in pain from his injured shoulder. It was obvious they were not fond of James any longer.

"We can't waste any time! We can't let him do this for nothing!" Amy spoke up from her crouched position.

As the guards led him toward the west building, we ran from our spot to the east building directly toward the gate that had remained open. We prayed that whoever monitored the cameras was occupied by watching James being taken away, giving us enough time to figure out how to enter. We ran in a crouched position as fast as we could to the corner of the east building, where only one camera stood in between Mandala and us. Once we reached the corner, we noticed a single door and many windows lining the wall. Of course, the door was locked shut, leaving our only opportunity as the windows.

"Check all the windows!" I whispered to Zeke and Amy.

"Does it smell like alcohol to you, guys?" Zeke asked as he checked the windows. Below the sixth window, we noticed that the grass was damp and did, in fact, smell of alcohol. "They must have poured their drink out through the window."

After checking five windows, the sixth one finally opened. We sighed in relief and then silenced ourselves as we tried to enter as quietly as possible.

Once we had all crawled through the window, we examined the room we entered that appeared to be some sort of office.

"Look what I found!" Zeke exclaimed in a hushed voice after rummaging through a desk drawer. "It's a map of the facility."

"Good, can you locate where we are exactly?" I asked as I moved over to the table.

It turned out that we were on the same floor as the server room, but we couldn't risk going out of the room to explore. The server room was in a 'Staff Only' room and was probably going to be guarded. We needed to go unnoticed until we could get Finn access to their computers. Zeke came up with a plan. He had now taken the lead over James as the senior individual of the group. Above us was a ventilation and power duct access grill, and according to the map, it led all the way to the server room, which was two rooms over. From there, I could gain access to a computer and plug in the flash drive. Amy produced a Swiss army knife from her pocket, which we used to unscrew the grill to the duct system. Zeke boosted me the same way he had done at Amy's house. It all seemed a lifetime ago; climbing through Amy's kitchen window seemed like child's play compared to this. This was even more dangerous than the previous entry since our discovery would mean the end of us and also the end to any thoughts of vengeance we could have dreamed of.

As I crawled through the vents, I was thankful for my physique. The space was narrow, and I barely had any wiggle room. I had to take extra precautions, as I did not know who was down below. Any scraping sound could draw unnecessary attention. Zeke had informed me the access grill to the server room was going to be the second one I would encounter in the duct.

Crawling through the vents soon had me dripping in sweat, and I was thankful for reaching the room quickly. I pulled out Amy's Swiss army knife and unscrewed the grill carefully, catching the screws before they could fall. If there was anyone nearby, I risked being discovered immediately. With sweaty fingers, I gently placed the grill to the side of the vent, careful not to make any clattering noise. I then peeped through the hole to check for anyone within the server room. The server room was dimly lit, and no one seemed to be around. I jumped down carefully and landed softly on the tips of my toes. I took in my surroundings. The room was filled with rows and rows of cabinets with wires sticking out of them. Pulsating lights of green and amber pierced the darkness of the room.

I gathered myself from the jump and turned on the nearest computer I could find. Finn had instructed me to plug the flash drive into the server computer and open the file that I had downloaded. I got to my feet and walked in the direction of the nearest aisle. As soon as I had entered, I heard an overhead clicking and buzzing sound. Immediately, the sound stopped, and the darkroom was flooded with white fluorescent light. The entire aisle was now properly visible.

"Shit," I mumbled under my breath.

The lights were motion activated. It seemed I was still in luck since the sudden illumination did not draw any attention.

"Lucas? Is that you Lucas?" A voice asked from somewhere in the room.

My heart began to race immediately. I was not the only one in the room. The man with the voice had gotten curious by the sudden illumination of the room, and he was now walking down the aisle of cabinets in my direction. The lights began to flick on as he walked down. I quickly got behind one of the cabinets, hoping I was going to stay unnoticed. Next to the cabinet where I was hiding, I noticed a fire extinguisher. It was heavier than I anticipated, but it was the only object that I could make use of. The outline of a man appeared from the aisle. He was looking in the other direction and was oblivious to my presence.

"Lucas quit playing games, would you?" He said again.

The man I was staring at was wearing a white coat over a pair of matching trousers and a shirt. He had short stature and was not taller than me by much. I slowly walked up to his back with instant regret of what I was about to do. He probably has no idea about what they do in the facility. Or, he does, and he's probably just as evil as the rest of them. Before I could come up with another reason for not going through, I raised the cylinder and struck it into the back of his head. His body crumpled as he fell unconscious. I had neutralized the threat and knew I had to make the best use of the time I had. There was nothing to restrain the now unconscious man, and even if I had, Lucas might be here any moment. I hurried over to the server computer. The lights flickered on and off as I walked briskly toward it. I sat in the seat in front of the computer, plugged in the flash, and followed Finn's instructions. As soon as the malware program was running, I fished out the micro earpiece from my pocket and dialed Finn on my mobile.

"Hey. I can see you've gained access to the server." Finn's voice came over the earpiece.

"Yeah. How long till you have control?"

"Two minutes."

"Good. I don't have much time. I had to knock out someone to get access to the server."

"Where are the others?"

"James acted as a decoy for us to get in. They have him in custody. I left the others in a room nearby, and I crawled through the vent to get into the server room."

"Okay. Is the room where the others are safe?"

"Yes."

"It's best you get back to them. By the time you get there, I'll have gotten full control. Don't forget to unplug the flash."

"Okay."

I unplugged the flash from the computer and made my way back to the access grill. The lights came on again as I walked by. The man was still unconscious. I was now faced with the difficulty of climbing up to the access duct. I looked around for anything that would bolster me up. The only thing that came to my mind was the chair at the computer desk. I went back to the desk and wheeled the chair over to the access point, now without a grill. My victim was still lying unconscious as I quickly climbed into the entrance using every ounce of strength I had.

With the tip of my feet, I pushed the chair away from the vent to keep them guessing for a while. I replaced the grill to the vent, but there was no way to screw it from the outside now. Apart from the missing grill screws, there was hardly any indication that someone came in through the vents. Even if they discovered what happened, later on, I hoped we were as far away as possible. The journey back to the room was as challenging as the previous one because I still needed to remain quiet. As soon as I got to the access grill of the office, I peeped in first to make sure everything was fine. Zeke's thumbs-up sign to me indicated we were in the clear. I plopped down from the vent and landed on the balls of my feet.

"How did it go?" Amy asked

"I ran into a staff member in the server room. He's unconscious, but we need to move fast."

Amy and Zeke stared at each other in disbelief as I recounted to them what happened. Finn's voice then came through the earpiece, telling me he had full access.

"Give me what you got," I whispered back to Finn.

Finn then explained the facility layout to me, and with the aid of the map Zeke had found, we drew up a quick plan. From the cameras in the facility, Finn could tell that there were children at the facility, and they were currently in a classroom. We planned to blend in with them until we got our chance to make it to the administrative block. The administrative block was where James was being held, according to Finn. We had to get to him in time and bring an end to this entire madness.

"Do you think the children here are held against their will, or do you think they know exactly what's happening?" Amy asked as we prepared to leave the room.

"I seriously doubt they know what's going on. I don't think they came here willingly. Why else the security and secrecy?" I replied. With Finn talking through my earpiece and the map, we navigated our way from the room and past a corridor with numbered doors. There was no sign of anyone around.

"The door to your left. Go in. It's a dormitory room you could get some clothes to wear, and you guys would blend in better that way." Finn said as soon as we got to the end of the corridor.

"It has some type of biometric key entry. How do we get in?" I asked. It seemed we had hit a dead end.

"Give me a sec." Came his reply. In the surrounding quietness, I could hear Finn typing through the earpiece. In my mind, I could visualize him at his desk at home, furiously typing away on the keyboard with a can of an energy drink next to his mouse. I hoped he didn't get in trouble for helping us. We waited in silence, and I was beginning to get nervous. My biggest fear was if someone came along. Or would the guy in the server room have regained consciousness? Would he have raised an alarm that an unknown person attacked him? My mind was racing again when a soft click sounded snapping me out of thinking. The door was open.

"Finn, you're a genius," I said as I pushed the door open wider.

We walked into the dormitory room. There were two bunk beds and clothes littered everywhere. We could immediately smell the alcohol coming from the closet. It looked to be the room of teenagers, causing us plenty of confusion. We approached the wardrobe door and cracked it slightly to assess the contents.

"Guys, we should change into their clothes," I said, following Finn's advice.

They agreed, and we immediately raided the closets and located uniforms that consisted of gray dress pants and a matching gray polo. Zeke quickly and quietly crossed the corridor to find a boy's room. Finn granted him access, and Zeke returned dressed in the same uniform.

When we all entered the hallway together, we saw a door that led up to the stairs.

"You have to go up, there's nothing down here," Finn stated.

As dangerous as it now seemed, I knew that nothing would be accomplished if we waited around the dorms. We could only guess what the company was doing to James by now. We couldn't waste another second. Neither Zeke nor Amy responded. Instead, they just followed my movements, and I followed Finn's instructions.

We entered the narrow, back stairwell, and noticed cameras above us. I motioned to Zeke and Amy to lower our heads as we made our way up the stairs. When we reached the top of the staircase, we peered out through the small glass window to check for anyone. We noticed no one and exited the dim stairwell. As soon as we exited the stairs, I lost connection with Finn. I quickly pulled out the phone from my pocket. To my utter dismay, there was no reception. It seemed they had jammed all cellular networks.

"Guys, we're on our own from here. No reception." I said as I placed the phone back in my pocket.

Chapter 22
The Torture

This hallway was different from the one downstairs. It appeared to be the hallway of a school and was so silent you could hear a pin drop.

"Maybe a class is in session?" Zeke suggested.

We shrugged our shoulders and moved further down the hallway until we finally heard an echoing voice as we approached. We reached a classroom at the end of the hallway and saw one teacher and one guard standing at the center of the round room, while the students circled them in rows of long tables that wrapped around a massive holographic screen that centered the room.

The room appeared in a futuristic manner. The long tables were silver, as well as the chairs. The large holographic screen even had a white glow to it, causing my eyes to strain. While the teacher and guard addressed the further side of the room with their backs faced toward the classroom door, we took our opportunity to enter and sit in the back row.

As we silently sat without the teacher or guard noticing, we received scared looks from our peers around us as if we took a very bold move in entering the class late. Teenage students surrounded us, who all had the looks of fear instilled into them. All of the students meshed together in their bland uniforms. Looks of exhaustion and drain overtook their faces.

"Today, we will be watching a video on torture. As usual, we will not be leaving until the last student stops crying. Expect today to be quite a long day." The teacher stared at a girl in the front with a smirk as he made his last comment. There was an empty seat next to her.

Was she known for crying the longest?

I exchanged perplexed looks with Zeke and Amy as the video was projected onto the holographic screen. It looked like a four-dimensional screen that wrapped around the center of the room for all of the students to view at a 360-degree rotation. It felt like the scene was happening inside the classroom with us. A teenage boy appeared on the screen strapped to a metal chair.

This wasn't a movie scene. This was a live video.

As soon as the students seemed to recognize who was on the screen, they gasped and mumbled to each other. The girl at the front was repeating, "No, no, no!" The boy on the screen had big brown eyes and messy outgrown brunette hair that shielded his eyes. He was clothed in the same gray uniform that everyone around us was dressed in, including me.

It looked like he had already been beaten fairly badly and had bruises forming on his arms and face. His tormentor towered over him and had a black mask on his face to disguise his identity. He did no talking. We all watched in horror and anticipation, as the tormentor began by ripping off the boy's fingernails and toenails one by one. He wasted no time. The boy screamed and pleaded to stop, but the tormentor continued without hesitation.

One by one, the students began to shed silent tears but quickly wiped them away before the teacher or guard noticed. Suddenly, the girl up front stood up while screaming through sobs. "Stop this! Stop this right now," she begged. She turned toward her fellow peers expecting them to help her, but no one moved from their seats, frozen with shock. The girl made eye contact with me, and although she blended in with the sea of gray, her soft honey-colored eyes struck me. I wanted so badly to help her, to help all of them, but I had to remind myself I was here for a larger purpose. The guard rushed toward her with a long black baton. He slashed her back while she screamed and forced her into her seat while handcuffing her hands to the chair.

As piercing as her screams were, no one dared to move.

Meanwhile, the torturer had just stabbed a knife into the poor boy's quadriceps. Blood oozed from his light gray pants. The sight was dreadful. Amy, Zeke, and I were horrified. What was going on here? Why did they want to prevent the students from crying at videos of torture? Given the chaos, there was absolutely no way to sneak out of the classroom now.

Tears began to stream from all of our faces. At this rate, nothing would get accomplished if we were all stuck in this room. We had no way of knowing how long the torture would last. Mumbles and hiccupped cries still echoed among the students. "Silence!" the teacher demanded. The mumbles quieted, but the sounds of sniffles and cries could still be heard. This was one of their own. They each imagined themselves in his place.

"Would they kill this poor boy?" I thought to myself. My tears were flowing even faster. My heart ached for the teenagers that surrounded me. It ached for my mother and uncle.

"Please! No!" the boy on the screen screamed, begging the man to stop. The man placed plyers around his pinky toe, and we all covered our eyes, knowing what would happen next.

The plyers clenched around his toe, causing blood to spew. The boy shook his leg in pain, screaming.

I couldn't watch this anymore.

And neither could the girl upfront.

The girl at the front began screaming at the top of her lungs. She didn't care what the consequences were anymore. That was clearly someone close to her, and they were mutilating him and making a show of it. She screamed and screamed with her eyes shut and her head thrown back. She cried as she was whipped and began slamming her head against the metal table. She wouldn't stop. She was hysterical.

We were all witnessing her breakdown. The company had stripped her of her dignity. We looked away from the horror on the screen to watch this heartbroken girl. The table became stained with cherry red blood that splattered from her forehead. Her scream was so high-pitched, we began covering our ears. Even though the teacher demanded to silence herself, she continued.

The whips from the guard became harder and more frequent. I noticed the slashes going higher and higher up her back and became worried he'd slash the back of her head. In that instance, my fear became true. He slashed her head during her final scream, causing her to fall silent immediately. Her head hit the table, ceasing anymore sounds in the room. Blood seeped through her light gray polo and through her dark brunette hair.

The teacher pulled out a walkie-talkie, "That's enough, Buck." He spoke with satisfaction.

We heard those words echo through the four-dimensional screen, causing the torturer to end harming the boy.

The teacher got what he wanted. He broke them both.

What appeared to be paramedics entered the room to collect the girl. The paramedics had stone-cold faces and shoved the stretcher ahead of them aggressively. Similar to all other staff in the building, they were dressed in white. However, these members were clothed in scrubs.

The girl was still unconscious as they halfheartedly put her on the stretcher. All of the students had halted their crying in the hope that they would finally be sent away, most likely to cry in private. The paramedics were out of the room as fast as they had come in. When they passed me to reach the door, I noticed a key card sticking out of the girl's now bloodied pants pocket. I quickly and carefully slid it out of the pocket as the paramedics struggled to shove the stretcher through the narrow doorway. Only Zeke and Amy noticed me.

"Alex and Brian," the teacher began. "Clean up this mess, and the rest of you be gone," he motioned to the girl's desk that was now covered in blood. The rest of the students scurried out of their seats and rushed to the door, so we followed. "What's the plan now?" Amy whispered as we crammed ourselves through the door.

"We have to get into one of their rooms to find out what's going on," Zeke concluded. We followed our fellow classmates down the stairs and back to the dormitories, while I pulled out the key card to examine it. It had the girl's picture on it with her name, Mayhem Greene, followed by a six-digit number just like James had. There was also a three-digit number that I assumed to be her room number.

"Come on guys, we have to find room 103."

As we were exiting the staircase, I noticed a familiar face surrounded by strawberry blonde hair.

I tugged Zeke's arm to get his attention. "Is that Felicity?" Zeke was just as shocked. How did she beat us here?

We ducked our heads in the crowd and headed in the opposite direction, hoping that we were going the right way to room 103.

There was a group of three girls in front of us that appeared timid and whispered amongst themselves as they headed to their room. We figured they were our best bet since they were in a group of three, and each room had space for four people.

We followed them, and as soon as they opened their room door to room 103, we rushed them in, closing the door behind us. "Sshhh!" I put a finger to my lips, taking in my surroundings. This was a different room than the one we had entered. Similar, but organized differently based on the people who inhabited it. The beds were neatly made, and the clothes weren't scattered anywhere.

It appeared to be quite clean compared to the other we had entered. The blinds were shut, casting a shadow across the room. Although it was daytime, it felt like the middle of the night. The only aspect that was distinctly similar to that of the other room was the furniture.

The girls all looked scared and confused, but a hint of hope gleamed in their eyes. It was obvious that none of the students in the class had ever seen us before, so why did no one speak up? Two of the girls sat together on a bottom bunk, holding each other. The taller girl wiped off her thick-framed glasses as if she couldn't actually tell if we were there or not. The third girl sat on a neatly made bottom bunk with her arms crossed. She had fire-red curly hair and freckles that dotted her pale skin. The contrast of her red hair on her plain gray attire reminded me of the blood from Mayhem that now stained the table. She looked distraught from the situation in the classroom that involved her roommate. I assumed the four girls must be close based on their defensive mannerisms. "We're here to help." I figured this was the best way to start off our conversation not to scare our new members away. They seemed to flinch at the word help. Was this what they were told when they were brought here? Has someone offered to help before?

"We're here to stop what's going on, but we need your help," I hoped that these were the right words to say. I hoped that these girls wanted out as badly as we wanted them out. They were young and had their entire lives ahead of them. They shouldn't be stuck in this futuristic box of horrific experiments.

"What is going on here? What did we just witness?" Zeke interrupted with brows furrowed. I guessed we were going for a good cop–bad cop show. I was sucked out of my thoughts as quickly as I had been drawn into them. He looked angry. I could see the sweat glistening against his dark complexion. I noticed Amy grab his hand. She knew that only she could calm him. Zeke's bursts of anger were unstoppable for anyone else. We had already found this out on our short trip together. Somehow, Zeke connected to Amy like family. "We're being desensitized," the shorter girl spoke up. Her bangs fell into her eyes, preventing us from having any eye contact. She uncomfortably looked at the tiled floor.

"Desensitized?" I was more confused than before now. Were they not being experimented on as we had been? What was Mandala's goal now? Desensitizing teenagers had to come with some sort of larger plan.

Everyone could read the confusion on my face; I was sure of it. It was obvious we were outsiders. My hands balled into fists, and my mind raced a mile a minute. James was still in danger. We needed to move quicker than this.

"That guy on the screen is one of our classmates that has always kind of rebelled. He and Maya are best friends," the redhead spoke up.

Maya? Mayhem's nickname, I assumed.

"Where did Mandala get you guys from? How is this happening?"

The girls explained how they had been kidnapped from a youth homeless shelter and brought to Mandala as pawns for his purposes. Mandala was recruiting kids and desensitizing them in order to send them back into society to do his dirty work. They were being sent out on missions to murder political figures to fill Mandala's agenda of rebuilding society to his favor.

Maybe "Felicity" had been sent out as well, I wondered. This was a dangerous situation. We needed to do something fast.

"How can we get to Mandala?" I was antsy now. I couldn't believe the lengths Mandala had gone for his stupid agenda. These poor children were suffering because of his quest for power. Too much time was going by, and I couldn't trust that James wasn't being harmed. For all we knew, he could be next on that holographic screen being tortured.

The fiery redhead explained that we needed a staff member's key card to get into the west building. This required her to find someone by the name of Isabella to come to our aid. A supposedly trusted source. She left the room to get her while we planned out our next moves. "So, Isabella will take us to the next building, and what are we supposed to do next?" Amy was making quick calculations in her head, doubting our success at even getting to the other building with no harm.

"I can help with that," the taller girl that I had come to know as Danielle, carefully displayed a small pipe to us.

"This is a pipe bomb. It won't do too much damage, but if you run into guards outside, just light it, and it'll buy you enough time to get inside." Zeke, Amy, and I were in awe. There was no extra time to ask how these young girls located the right materials to produce a bomb, but we were inherently grateful.

The redhead returned with another girl who was closer in age to me. She had wide-set eyes, a slackened face, and a bloody bottom lip from biting it nervously. She introduced herself as Isabella with a nervous handshake to accompany her. We explained to her that we were in a hurry, so she quickly described the blueprints of the west building.

"Mayhem and Caleb are most likely both in the medical wing, which is the first door on the right. I trust them, they've been communicating with me since they arrived here with plans to escape, but they are not in the best condition right now. Mandala's office is upstairs at the very end of the hall of the west building. Your friend is probably being questioned and tortured in the basement of the west building." Everyone being in different areas was not helping our time limit. As much as we regretted admitting this, we realized we needed to split up.

Isabella agreed to go to the medical wing to help Maya and Caleb, while Zeke and Amy decided to go straight to Mandala's office, leaving me to find James. The girls produced a box of matches for the pipe bomb and wished us luck. Their jobs were to create a distraction in the east building to draw as many staff as they could, away from the west building. They were going to set off another pipe bomb in the public bathrooms.

"The girls mentioned that Mandala is trying to rebuild society. What kind of society is he trying to create?" Amy spoke calmly to Isabella, if not for herself, for Zeke's sake. In turn, she had decided to care for Zeke too. "All of the experiments he's conducted over the years were to create his own breed of people that can overthrow the hierarchy of today's society. He wanted to be in control. He failed with the experiments on the babies, thinking that he could formulate diseases to work in his favor by altering genes. He hoped to create stronger humans that couldn't feel pain, couldn't get sick, and couldn't feel emotions. He ended up giving the babies life-threatening diseases, which caused him to change routes and focus his efforts on ending emotions, which he considers a form of suffering. Mandala doesn't believe that power moves can be made if you have emotions. He has convinced himself that he really can change the world."

The pieces of the puzzle began to make sense now. I was never able to comprehend Mandala's reasoning for experimenting on anyone fully, let alone babies. The answer brought me more skepticism about my mother and James' morals. We parted ways from the girls, as Isabella led us outside using her key card at the door. The spring air was crisp and smelled of freshly mowed grass. They quietly crossed the walkway, being wary of guards. From the walkway up above them, there were shouts.

"Who's down there? We're on lockdown." Guards covered every inch of the upstairs walkway and were now leaning over the railing to see who had dared to walk outside during a lockdown. Meanwhile, my match was being lit, and a swift toss upstairs caused an explosion and a commotion that would buy us time. Isabella nervously swiped us into the west building, and we all went our separate ways. I immediately took the stairwell down, while she entered the first room in the building, and Zeke and Amy took the staircase upstairs.

Chapter 23
The Truth

As I made my way down the dimly lit staircase, my stomach knotted in unease. I wasn't sure what I would be walking into, and couldn't bear the thought of losing James a second time. He had played such a significant role in my life, and he had indeed re-entered for a greater purpose. As much as it pained me to be able to forgive him after leaving us, I understood his reasons for wanting to protect us. I couldn't imagine anything happening to him here at the company that started this entire mess.

At the bottom of the staircase was a large, heavy metal door. I couldn't hear or see anything beyond it. There was no way I would be able to sneak into this room. I had to make myself vulnerable, which I wasn't sure would necessarily benefit James. I was unarmed, weaponless, and afraid. Afraid for myself and for James. Before I had another moment to reconsider what I was doing, I shoved the door open.

There, in the middle of the room, sat James, tied to a metal chair just as the boy had been on the screen. There were blood splatters left all over from past tortures stained to the floor and walls. The room smelled rotten, and a single light flickered overhead. It was a place that made the hairs on my skin rise. A place I didn't want to be in. I hurried over to him, trying to figure out a way to free him from the chair. My eyes frantically looked around for a sharp object to cut the bounds.

James' eyes found me with instant fear. "Alice, get out of here," his demand came out weak and distant. His voice was giving up. "Mandala." James' eyes weren't on me anymore. He readjusted himself in the chair, and his body stiffened at the sight of the man that had entered the room.

It was an older man. His hair coated in silver seemed to mirror the metal that furnished the buildings. He held a devilish smirk and was dressed in an all-white crisp suit. This was the man who had started it all. His presence filled me with dread. It reeked of so much evil. "Welcome back, James." He clasped his hands together as he admired the damage done to James' body as if it were his own masterpiece. Behind him were several guards, I gulped. I was surrounded. I had walked into a trap. "And I suppose this is... Felicity's daughter." He turned to face me with a wide grin. I looked at him with disgust and spat in his face without regard to any consequences. The sound of my mother's name on his lips infuriated me to the point I was shaking. No longer was I scared, instead I was enraged at this animal and what he had done over the years.

In an instant, I was slapped across the face. My cheek felt numb under his heavy hand, and I could only feel the heat rise to my cheeks. James attempted to jump out of his chair but to no avail, considering his hands and feet were zip-tied to the indestructible metal chair.

The guards reached for me and struggled to strap me to a chair, given my resistance. They finally managed to hold my wrists and legs down, as they bound me with zip ties across from James. "Well let's get to it. You're obviously here because of Felicity's death." He was blunt and seemed rushed like he didn't care to explain his actions to someone like me. "Why did you kill her?" I was seething. I was now facing the man whose hands were responsible for the death of my innocent mother.

Mandala shrugged. "Felicity, your mother, couldn't just let things be, as stubborn as she was. We knew of her plans to expose the company, so we had to dispose of her properly." Dispose of her properly? With a knife? Displayed on the kitchen floor for me to discover?

"So everyone that you killed-"

"They were all on the verge of exposing my company that I have taken decades to build." He concluded my sentence, implying that it was his only obvious option to kill all those innocent people. "They thought they could get the best of me, reveal my magnificent intentions to the world when the world is not ready for it. But amongst them, there is always a traitor. They are all dead now. Every one of them. And so should all of you. My mistakes must be erased."

I was in disbelief that someone could be so careless and cruel toward human lives. Toward babies too. I thought about the file on my computer that Finn now held access too. I wondered if curiosity got the best of him and he had opened it yet. We were interrupted when guards entered the room with Amy and Zeke bound and chained. "Felicity" trailed behind them. They were forced into seats just as I had been. I was highly disappointed that we had all been caught. Was this how it was going to end? With all of us killed by this monster? Would he win again? I made direct eye contact with the stranger I had met in the library. She looked younger in her gray uniform and less intimidating. I glanced down to see my ring on her finger. The ring that her partner had taken at my mother's funeral. The girl appeared to be apologizing to me with her eyes. Her body was shivering, even though it wasn't cold. There wasn't even a breeze down here. She had caught Amy and Zeke and delivered them to Mandala. Mandala nodded towards her, pleased, and she disappeared.

This moment made me realize how this young girl had been so badly manipulated. It was obvious she was willing to do anything she could to survive. Her mannerisms indicated to me that she was filled with regret, although I'm sure she assumed her success would give her some freedom in the prison in which she was being held captive.

"Welcome home, everyone." Mandala was taking so much joy out of this. He was able to witness his test subjects at such an old age. He seemed surprised to see that we had survived and lived relatively normal lives. I knew he had questions for us, but I had no intent to answer. I looked around the room. My uncle, James, was in bad shape. If he didn't get any help, he was going to die just like my mother. I knew a worse fate was going to meet Amy, Zeke, and me. I couldn't let this man win again. He had caused enough pain.

Somehow, the adrenaline that rushed through my body allowed me to stand at a bent angle, still attached to the chair. The zip ties were cutting off the circulation in my legs as they slid up my ankles to allow me to be able to stand. I immediately rushed into Mandala with all of my might pinning him down to the floor.

He groaned in pain, but before I could continue, I was being beaten by batons from several guards. My body was taking blows to my stomach, back, and limbs. Every inch of me.

Did these idiots not know I can't feel pain?

I endured their blows until Mandala finally signaled for them to stop. Bruises immediately began forming, and blood dripped from freshly open cuts.

"She can't feel it." Mandala reminded the guards of my disease as he gathered himself.

This caused the guards to have the realization that in order to hurt me, James should be their target.

They charged at James with their batons swinging, as I shouted for them to stop.

"No, stop! Please! Uncle James!"

A sentence that would change my life forever.

Mandala ceased the attack at the sound of my voice. "Did you say 'uncle'?" He questioned with a gleaming curiosity. Something wasn't right.

I gave no response as I looked for James' eyes for any clue as to what was going on. A look of guilt encompassed him.

"You thought James was your uncle, this entire time?" Mandala was nearly cackling. Something had him in shock.

"Alice." I felt Mandala's eyes on me as he tried to read me for a reaction.

"James is your father."

I was stunned. I couldn't react. James? My father?

Why would this be hidden from me? And for so long? I didn't know what to feel. My entire life had gone by with the assumption that my father was dead. That my deceased father had left me his Firebird. James' five-year disappearance now hurt so much more. How could he leave his wife and daughter for that long? Nothing was making sense to me. Why had he and my mother lied to me all these years? Growing up, I had always wanted a father. It was ironic that my "uncle" James had played that role so well that when he had left, I was once again reminded that I had no father. And now this? I didn't even know what questions I could ask to help me to understand.

Zeke and Amy looked just as stunned, but Amy, for different reasons.

Before I had any time to take in the reality of what my life had become, Amy did the one thing that I had been praying wouldn't happen this entire journey.

She forgot.

Chapter 24
Alice

"Where am I?"

"Who are you, people?"

"Why am I tied up?"

Amy was panicking. Her head bobbed as she took in her surroundings, trying to find any sense of familiarity. Her Alzheimer's had set in, and none of us would be able to find a way to explain any of this to her.

"Amy, Amy, calm down. It's me, Zeke." Zeke's bound wrists couldn't find a way to grasp Amy's hands. The guards stood back, unsure of how to handle the situation. They had been trained to hit, and this was an entirely unfamiliar situation to them.

She became hysterical. Imagine waking up in a basement, bound to a chair by zip ties, and surrounded by guards with batons. "Somebody help me! Where am I?" She was crying and shaking up and down, trying to free herself from the restraints of the metal chair. Tears streamed down Zeke's face as he continued trying to calm her. "Amy, I'm right here, it's okay. It's Zeke." His attempts were useless.

As much as he had previously joked about how 'Amy with Alzheimer's' would be no help, he was falling for her. Her illness would tear him apart, just as much as it had done to her. Zeke had grown to love Amy, and dealing with Alzheimer's in such a situation was truly heartbreaking.

Everything was happening incredibly fast.

Nothing was being processed in my consciousness anymore. I looked around at all of the faces in the room, but they were becoming fuzzy, unrecognizable. I heard muffled shouts from James, in-between my hyperventilation. I heard cries for help from Amy and Zeke. I was trying to call out to them, but my mind was dark. When my stomach gave out, I knew I was clocking out.

My intestines were suddenly on fire with a feeling that was foreign to me. Nausea slowly crept up, and I felt the color diminish from my face. My mind was gliding through an unfilled space accompanied by a thick static. My pulse echoed beyond my chest wall, resounding in my ears. My own thumping heartbeat was the only sound I could make out. It was causing an overwhelming amount of pressure to try to remain awake. Trying to fight the darkness that was consuming me was exhausting, and eventually, I couldn't hold on anymore. My body was depleting away.

Something that I couldn't understand was happening to my body. The whacks from the baton were far more lethal than I had anticipated. The damage was done to me internally. I had outstayed my life expectancy. My entire life had felt like a race while living with congenital insensitivity.

My disease had finally caught up to me, too.

PART FOUR

Chapter 25
The After

Maya awoke on a cold metal table to bright fluorescent lights and Isabella's tormented expression peering down on her. It took her a second to focus her swollen eyes on the white room. She looked to her surroundings and recognized the medical wing that she had become so accustomed to.

In this place, she had gotten her steady supply of pain medications and also where she stole various chemicals for pipe bombs. This was the place where her story began at Mandala and the place where her story would end. She tried to create a wall in her mind to shut her out from the pain she had gone through.

And most of all, to shut herself out from watching Caleb be tortured, which had killed her over and over. Her friend didn't deserve what had happened to him. He had to be dead, and this sent a wave of sadness all over her body. However, she could only hope for the better. If she was alive, perhaps he could be alive. Perhaps…Once she readjusted herself, she realized she didn't know the condition Caleb was in, causing her to jolt upright. This sudden movement did not help her pounding headache, and she brought her hands to her forehead, trying to locate the source of the pain. Her body ached where each whack of the baton had struck her. She felt dried blood on the back of her head.

"Where is he?" She mumbled to Isabella. Isabella knew who she was referring to. Everyone had come to understand that Maya and Caleb were inseparable.

"He's doing better. He's stable now," she pointed with her eyes to a bed that was across the room. Caleb's entire body seemed to be wrapped in bandages and casts. For a change, his eyelids were purple instead of his fists. Isabella grabbed Maya's shaky hands and helped her down from the table. She carefully walked her over to him. He was alive! Her Caleb was alive! Mandala probably had worse plans for them, but all that mattered at the moment was that her best friend was alive. Her future scared her, but...

Maya suddenly noticed the swarms of police officers enclosed the medical wing. "What's going on?" Maya asked on their way over to an unconscious Caleb. There was so much commotion that Maya's ears began to ring. She could hear gunshots, screams, and sirens.

"The authorities are here. Someone must have tipped them off. Mandala will be shut down by nightfall." Isabella's words came out smooth like butter to Maya. Tears filled the brims of her eyes out of pure happiness. She didn't think that this day would ever come. Someone named Finn had initiated the call to the police, which led to the rescue of the residents at the facility.

Even in her unconsciousness after being attacked, she had totally given up on them ever being rescued. Seeing Caleb get tortured had made her promise herself, never to try to escape again. Remaining here and carrying out Mandala's will was what she would do to avoid herself and Caleb from getting hurt again. But now, help had come. It didn't matter that it had arrived late.

The door opened, and two doctors who she didn't recognize hurried into the room. Letting go of her, Isabella went over to them. They prodded over Caleb, her eyes attentive as she tried to hear what they were saying in whispers about him. Her friend was in terrible shape, but Caleb was a fighter, and she trusted him to fight this.

"How's Caleb?" Maya asked, unable to take their silence anymore.

"He will be fine. He had some traumatic injuries, but he's out of danger for now. He's in an induced sleep, but he will be awake soon," one of the doctors explained. Once she was reunited with Caleb and assured by doctors not associated with Mandala that he would have a slow but full recovery, Maya finally felt whole again.

Her Caleb was alive. Perhaps, things would never go back as they were, but all that mattered was that he was alive. She sat by his bedside, not willing to leave him until the doctors cajoled her away, insisting she needed to rest as well. It took over an hour before the commotion stopped. Walking beside Isabella and Caleb, who was on a stretcher, they passed through the hallways. It looked like a hurricane had gone through the building.

The walls had been torn apart, filled with bullet holes. Papers and files covered the ground, and furniture had been thrown over. The cops had brought with them chaos, which had been unleashed on the company. Her eyes rested a couple of times on the bodies who wore the white uniform Mandala's guards wore. She felt no pity for these men and women who had hurt her and the other children in several ways. They emerged into the sunlight, and she took a deep breath of freedom. In a line were many handcuffed staff members and guards, most of whom she recognized, with furious cops monitoring them. There was also a bus that the children were being led into by a few officers. As much as she wanted to be with the others, and know all that had happened, she couldn't leave Caleb. She needed to be with him. She had to be there when he woke up. Paramedics were putting Caleb on a stretcher to be transported via helicopter to a nearby hospital. She couldn't go with them on the helicopter, but she would go with the cops to the hospital.

"Excuse me?" Maya tugged on the jacket sleeve of a passing officer. "Where are we?"

The officer looked at her with a mixture of pity and disbelief. "We're in Litchfield, New York," he watched Maya's expression for a reaction.

They had driven hours north from the homeless shelter.

It was now Isabella's turn to ask questions. "How are Alice, Amy, Zeke, and James?" Her confidence had grown since the news of Mandala's arrest. Her once timid shell was now cracking. She was easing into her newfound freedom.

The names were foreign to Maya. How much had happened since the classroom? She looked to Isabella for an answer but was met with an impatient set of eyes that told her "later." The officer had a regretful stare as he explained the status of the four names.

"Alice didn't make it." The words struck Maya as if she had known the girl herself. He explained that Alice had suffered major internal bleeding, leading to her death. Alice had congenital insensitivity preventing her from feeling pain and knowing that anything was wrong. The officer comforted Isabella by reminding her that Alice had survived as long as she could with the disease. Isabella's hands formed into fists, and she nodded for the officer to continue.

In all his years of active service, Officer Jones had never come across such a crime scene. It was one which he knew he would always remember. Just like the rest of his colleagues, he was trying to rein his anger in; otherwise, it would be taken out on the guards and workers of Mandala who were needed for bringing down others who had sponsored Mandala's works. To think this had been happening in his backyard for so long, without anyone suspecting what the scientist had been doing. He could not believe that anyone would hurt innocent and harmless children. He had seen what the monsters had done, and he so badly wanted to hurt them back. He had children of his own, and he could not imagine them being hurt in such a horrible way. At least the bastard would be behind bars now. He was the one who arrested him, and he took pride in that. He only hoped that one way or another, the children would be able to recover from what they had gone through. They would be rehabilitated and put in foster homes. It might do some good, but his years in the system didn't give him that much faith.

"Amy had an episode." Her Alzheimer's had set in, causing a frenzy and her need to be sedated. She would be flown along with Caleb to the hospital for immediate treatment and oversight.

"And Zeke?" Isabella asked. She had spent just a few moments with the trio, but she had felt so much pity for them. They had looked wounded and troubled, willing to put an end to Mandala and his ways. To know that Mandala had taken advantage of them when they were babies was heart-breaking. He hadn't cared about their future. He had not bothered that he was ruining their lives. All he had wanted was for his crazy dreams to come into manifestation. Because of him, the children, and now adults, were going through a painful life. Alice had looked like she was full of life. She had looked determined, and now she was gone. Perhaps, that was what she really needed. A way out of the painful world which had never treated her well. A world full of monsters.

"Zeke is okay. He didn't obtain any concerning injuries aside from bruises and cuts. He will be going along with Amy. According to him, he knows her best, and she needs him around. We're keeping a close watch on him, and we will have to go over his statement later on," the officer informed.

James was escorted out of one of the buildings handcuffed. He had a sad look as he was shoved into a police van. His heart was broken, and he knew he would never recover. In just a matter of months, he had lost two women who meant the world to him. He wished so much that he could have them back, but they were gone. First had been Felicity whom he loved, but had to leave for her safety. Then it was Alice. He regretted not telling her the truth, but they had thought it was the best for her. His little girl, who was such a fighter, was gone. Tears welled in his eyes, and his shoulders slumped in defeat. He should have protected his daughter more. Perhaps, he should never have given in on her quest to avenge Felicity and end the company. Then, he wouldn't have lost her. But would they have kept on living in fear that someday Mandala would come for them? Although the criminal was in custody, he wished he had not lost Alice in the process.

The door slammed in his face, and he rested on the backseat, several thoughts going through his mind. He had been arrested for his prior involvement with Mandala. Although his efforts to take down the company were not in vain, he knew there were legal matters now involved that would lead to his potential trial in court. However, to James, avenging Felicity was a success. Perhaps, if he got a good lawyer, he would get fewer years. Whatever happened, he took solace that Mandala would hurt no one again. His reign of terror was over.

Maya was still disoriented as she tried to process all of the information being thrown at her. So many misfortunes had happened to these unknown names. Maya wasn't ready to tell the world about the experiment that had been performed on her. Knowing that Amy and Zeke would be taken away for further testing, caused more internal panic. She didn't want to continue being a puppet for the government.

"Isabella, we can't tell them what they did to me," she whispered with wild eyes. The officer walked away to take care of more pressing matters, leaving Isabella and Maya at the foot of Caleb's bed.

Isabella nodded her head. She knew better. Her stay at Mandala caused her to be more cautious of people's best interests. Everyone had an ulterior motive now. If anyone found out about Maya, she would be taken away and tested like a lab rat. "What happened? Who was the officer talking about?" After Maya had cleared up her personal matters, she was drawn back to the reality of the situation.

"Alice, Amy, and Zeke were all subjects of Mandala's earlier experiments years ago. They came with James, who used to work here, to try to put an end to the company,"

Isabella sighed. It was obvious she felt conflicted. She wanted to feel overjoyed from their success in shutting down Mandala, but how could she when the people who helped end the company weren't even here to enjoy the satisfaction with her.

Mandala had pulled her away from her life. From school. From friends and family. Isabella's mind was at a standstill. She didn't know how she would be able to resume and go back to normal.

Maya held Caleb's limp hand and waited for the paramedics to take him away. She didn't know where they would go after all of this. How would they get back to Maryland? What shelter would they stay at next? The future was filled with unknowns, but only one thing was certain.

Mandala would never be a part of their lives ever again.

ALINA HASAN

The Epilogue

In through the nose, out through the mouth.

The crunchy lifeless autumn leaves that littered the trail made the bottoms of Maya's sneakers slippery. She was losing traction but was more determined to make it to the end and beat her personal record. Her shoes hit the ground quicker each time she landed, gaining speed as she neared the end. The trail was surrounded by woods on both sides, with no signs of civilization remotely nearby. Being alone deep in the woods on a "trail" created by her own footprints offered her no solace. At this hour, the slightest sounds from the woods gave her goosebumps. The anxious feeling in the pit of her gut forced her forward at record-breaking speeds. The reds had turned to browns, and the trees shivered in the cold from their bareness.

Mile marker 24.

In through the nose, out through the mouth.

Winter was approaching. Dusk was beginning to settle. The darkening skies offered no warmth from the disappearing sun. The wind was picking up and doing dances in the air. It seemed to be whispering in Maya's ear, "Don't forget."

Mile marker 25.

In through the nose, out through the mouth.

How could Maya forget? It was almost a year since Maya and Caleb had been kidnapped from the homeless shelter and taken to Mandala. Almost a year since Maya and Caleb had endured such traumatizing events. Almost a year since Maya had been experimented on. The mental wounds reopened every single day; time, unheeding of popular discourse, did not seem to heal this pain. Closure was never an option when there were still moles scattered throughout the real world that hadn't been caught by any police forces.

Sure, Mandala was in prison, rotting for a full life sentence with no chance of parole. But who knew what he was capable of even from behind bars? His connections exceeded everyone's beliefs. The foundation he had built his company on was a contentious political stance that had become popular enough to afford him followers. No one was safe. Maya wasn't safe. She was sure the others that had survived the company's collapse knew of her genetic changes and that it would only be a matter of time before they found her. She was also aware that Derek, the notorious betrayer, was still out in the world, probably continuing to serve as a mole for Mandala.

Mile marker 26.

"What's my time?" Maya slicked back her ponytail and began chugging the water bottle Caleb had waiting for her at the finish line.

"Two hours, five minutes. You are absolutely insane. That's only four minutes from the world record, and I can guarantee you didn't train nearly as much as that poor bastard."

Maya smirked. She knew Caleb was right but was too distracted by her endorphin high to have any sympathy for that marathon runner. All the endorphins exploding throughout her body left her speechless.

They both knew that it was out of the question for Maya to ever compete in a marathon. She was built competitively, and with her new capabilities and impressive speed, her time would be sure to raise questions.

"Come on, let's head back to the car." Caleb tossed her a banana to fuel up on as they continued down the trail to the parking lot.

Caleb was quiet on their walk back. The winter was reminding him of the old times too.

Their lives post-Mandala weren't too bad. They made enough cash for an apartment by doing odd jobs and using Maya's physical capabilities to their advantage. Isabella also moved in and went back to college. They had managed to stay off of the government's radar and were now easing back into society. And in the brief moments when, through the fog of fear and exhaustion, they were able to find intimacy and tenderness in each other, it all seemed worth it.

They did, however, have to remain unknown. Hidden from operatives of Mandala. After all of the arrests were made, a staff member revealed information about underground bunkers placed around the world serving Mandala's purpose. The staff member had hoped for a reduced sentence, but with no knowledge about where these so-called underground bunkers were, the information went unnoticed. Though Maya knew better. This news brought greater wariness to Maya, Caleb, and Isabella. If there were more locations, she was sure they knew about the experiments performed on her. Paranoia struck every one of her nerves - a constant companion.

She knew Isabella shared her panic; the girl woke up, screaming, from nightmares on a fairly regular basis. As for Caleb, if he felt the same paranoia she did, he never mentioned it. Perhaps he didn't want to stoke her terror, but Maya couldn't stop the same thoughts running through her head, over and over.

What if they were found? Her powers discovered? Where would they run?

Maya glanced at Caleb. In the past year, he had healed well from his injuries, but you could still see the toll they had taken on him. You could see it in his gait, in the way he carried himself. His physical scars had receded, but the mental ones remained.

He was scared too, even if he wouldn't admit it.

How long would they live like this? Constantly looking over their shoulders for a boogeyman? Maya was already so fatigued by it all, the idea of remaining in this state of constant dread and anxiety.

Isabella met them at the doorstep with a small smile. Maya could see the bags under her eyes, evidence of another sleepless night. She shot another glance at Caleb, noting the white that had sprung up in his hair.

No, they couldn't go on like this forever - a grim determination set in her heart.

The hunted would become the hunter.

They needed to find Derek.

THE NEW BREED

www.ingramcontent.com/pod-product-compliance
Lightning Source LLC
Chambersburg PA
CBHW030819090426
42737CB00009B/790